Easy

Easy

Chris Baber

Simply
delicious
home
cooking

EBURY
PRESS

Contents

Introduction

A Bit about Me

I've had a passion for cooking ever since I can remember.

Growing up in a small town in Northumberland, I'd come in from school and make dinner for the family most nights. I started off like most kids learning their way around the kitchen, mastering the classics like a good spag bol and trying new things when my confidence grew. A few of those early experiments, developed over time, have even made it into this book (you can thank my family for road-testing the earliest versions of the Arrabbiata sausage traybake). It's the way food brings people together and makes them happy that made me fall in love with cooking in those early days. I've always enjoyed the process, something I definitely get from my grandad; every time we went over for food, he'd be in the kitchen singing away to the radio having a right good time doing it. He showed me that cooking isn't just about the end goal, it's an experience and the act of cooking can be just as satisfying as the act of eating. To this day, when I'm cooking at home, the first step in any of my recipes is to get the music going. The more you enjoy it, the more you'll do it.

My love for cooking didn't end in my family kitchen up north though. I began sharing my recipes online in 2016 for fun, taking photos of my dinner and banging it on social media for no real reason other than wanting to share good food with people and to make the kitchen feel accessible for anyone. Later that year I went on to win BBC's show for home cooks, *Yes Chef*. One of my food heroes, Atul Kochhar, was a judge during my run on the show and he offered me a job with him in his Michelin star restaurant in Mayfair. As a passionate home cook, I never aspired to work in a restaurant but two weeks later I found myself working in one of the best places to eat in London, which was definitely a pinch-me moment, to say the least. After several months working alongside one of the best chefs in the business, I made the decision to leave to work on my true passion of inspiring people to cook at home. Taking everything I learned with Atul, I aspired to bring those skills into the home kitchens of the nation. With Atul's full support, I revved up my Instagram again and remembered just how much I had missed spending time interacting with the community I'd built before *Yes Chef*, and how rewarding it was to help people fall in love with cooking. There's nothing quite like hearing from a young family saying they made a recipe of mine and it has become a family favourite – even their fussy eaters were eating all the veg!

My passion for helping the nation find their feet in the kitchen really kicked off when I became an ambassador for Marks & Spencer food. Not just any job! My work with them is all about creating delicious family recipes for people to make at home, celebrating fresh ingredients and fuss-free delicious cooking. Over the last couple of years, I've

toured the UK from Scotland to Jersey with M&S, visiting their Select Farms and really getting to grips with all types of British produce. I'm constantly blown away by how much passion our farmers have and their drive to produce the best quality ingredients possible. It's a way of life and a labour of love. I've learned so much about seasonal British produce working with these incredible farmers, and their lovingly produced ingredients have inspired the recipes I create with M&S, but also many of the dishes in this book. It's not hard to create delicious food with good ingredients – quality over quantity is the key to easy cooking. I have had the joy of eating asparagus straight from the soil in the Wye Valley, cooking salmon overlooking the loch they were caught in and making cheese toasties for dairy farmers by the stunning Cornish coastline. I promise you there's nothing better than fresh-out-of-the-earth asparagus spears in the spring or getting your teeth sunk into the first cherries of summer. Our seasons may be short, but each one brings its own delicious produce.

It would be impossible to talk about my journey creating this book without mentioning the coronavirus pandemic. The lockdowns were tough, but I didn't want restrictions to stop people having access to a good dinner and so I launched two online cooking series. The first was a celeb live cookalong series, where I whipped up my recipes with some of the biggest names in the UK, from Gok Wan and Paddy McGuinness to Lisa Snowdon and Tom Daley. Then, for three days a week I hosted free online cookalongs for kids and

families. So many people said it was the first time they had cooked together as a family and often the first meal the kids had ever cooked from scratch. To see a family sharing pictures of themselves around the table tucking into food they had made with me was a highlight of my career. It was proper family grub, the sort of stuff you want for dinner night after night. Fuss-free, moreish food for even the newest of home cooks. I saw first-hand the positive impact that cooking together had for so many people and the joy a good evening stint by the hob could bring to people even at the hardest of times. And so, the idea for *Easy* was born. No trends or fads, just proper home cooking for everyone, to be made by anyone.

I've snuck in some of my own family's favourites, crowd-pleasers from those lockdown Instagram live sessions and even a few from my work with M&S, inspired by those incredible farmers bringing fresh food to our plates every day.

By the end of the book, I hope you'll have a few new favourite go-to dinners as well as the confidence to open the fridge and rustle something up without a recipe. Cooking is best when done together, so tag me and join the **#BaberFlavour** family when you share your cook up pictures on Instagram. Right, stick the radio on and let's get cooking.

Chris x

It's the way food brings people together and makes them happy that made me fall in love with cooking in those early days. I've always enjoyed the process, something I definitely get from my grandad; every time we went over for food, he'd be in the kitchen singing away to the radio having a right good time doing it. He showed me that cooking isn't just about the end goal, it's an experience and the act of cooking can be just as satisfying as the act of eating.

Chris Baber

Before you get cooking

This book is packed full of tasty recipes easy enough for a novice cook. It'll give you confidence in the kitchen and show you that no matter your ability right now, you can become a brilliant home cook. Trust me. There's nowt fancy about what we'll be doing here. It's proper grub. Too many recipes have you chasing around different shops, following complicated methods with overly fussy language. There's none of that here. My Easy recipe promise:

Easy to follow
All recipes are broken down into a simple step-by-step process with a clear (and honest!) cooking time for each recipe, starting at step 1 until the food is on the plate.

Easy to read
I've ditched any fancy cooking jargon and written everything in clear language everyone can understand.

Easy to find
You'll get everything from a supermarket, so there's no frantically running around ten different shops to make one recipe!

Easy to make
There's nothing fancy needed for these dishes, just the basics. I've included a kit list for you on page 16.

Getting started

Make time There's no need to rush. Each recipe has a cooking time. Pick a recipe you know you'll have enough time to comfortably make. I have been generous with the time, so if you're handy in the kitchen you'll fly through it.

Read the recipe
Read through from start to finish before you begin. Get clear on what you'll be doing so nothing comes as a surprise.

Prep, prep, prep
Get everything ready and prepped before you begin. Allow ten minutes or so to do all the chopping, get the ingredients to hand as well as having pots and pans out before turning on the gas.

Keep tidy
My top tip is to have a bowl on the counter to put any waste in. Things like your onion peel and garlic skin. Tidy as you go. When you're finished with something, put it straight back. Keep the decks clear. This means less tidying after dinner!

Have fun
Make time to cook. Get the radio or a favourite playlist on as job number one.

Be confident
If there's something you've not made before, get stuck in and give it a try. Take your time. Practice makes perfect!

A note on seasoning

Getting the seasoning right can be the difference between average and awesome.

Salt

Salt is a mineral that amplifies flavour. Adding it at the right time during cooking makes a massive difference to the end result and it's a simple skill worth mastering. Adding salt will enhance the flavour of a dish but can also change the texture of food as you cook, so it's important to add it at the right time during the cooking process and understand that popping it on at the very end might lead to a very different dinner.

Pepper

This is a spice, and it's not always needed at the same time as salt. When to add it entirely depends on the dish, and often on the type of cuisine you're cooking. This just means add a little, have a taste and keep doing it until it's right for you. Don't forget you can always add more but can't take it away. Taste your food as you're cooking (unless there's raw meat involved, of course) and adjust before you serve.

Salt & pepper aren't your only friends in the flavour game, you can also add things like lemon or vinegar for acidity or honey for sweetness. The key? Understanding what tastes good to you and going from there.

Easy kitchen tips

Chopping chicken & meat

Use kitchen scissors to cut chicken breasts and meat. Chop it straight into the pack it came in. This saves washing up a chopping board and a bowl.

Peeling ginger

Scrape the ginger with a teaspoon to easily remove the skin.

Peeling garlic

When peeling garlic, place the garlic on a chopping board, then give it a good bash with the heel of your hand. The skin will pop off easily.

Use your freezer

This will save time and money.

Make fresh herb ice cubes

Chop leftover herbs and put them in an ice-cube tray with water. You can then add them to recipes. You can also freeze chillies and usethem straight from frozen! They can be frozen whole, chopped or grated.

Freeze cheese

Grate it into a freezer bag or wrap it tightly in clingfilm.

Freeze bread

Store it in a freezer bag. You can toast it from frozen.

Shop smart & plan

Make a meal plan for the whole week or a few days at a time. This is a great way to save time and money and reduce food waste.

Love leftovers

I like to eat any leftovers for lunch the next day, or if I've made a big batch, I reheat it for dinner the next night. The recipes here are so good you won't have any problems eating them two nights in a row. Foods like a curry or stew freeze really well, so you can easily freeze individual portions for a homemade ready meal when time or money is a bit tight. My top tip is to label and date anything you freeze.

If you have any veg looking sorry for itself, or leftover rice from a curry, try my Spiced veggie pilaf (see page 136). Leftover roast chicken is great used in my Bang bang chicken salad (see page 48) or added to Singapore noodles (see page 122)! No leftovers need to be left behind.

My storecupboard essentials

Having a well-stocked cupboard is the first step to kitchen success, and means you'll only ever need to stock up on a few fresh ingredients before getting started on supper.

Pasta
Spaghetti – penne – fusilli
I always have a few types of pasta at home. Specific recipes call for different pasta shapes as they hold sauces in different ways, which can have an impact on taste. However, it's definitely not the end of the world if you end up using one over another at home. Always make the most of what you have.

Rice
Basmati – long-grain - risotto - paella – microwave rice
Basmati and long-grain rice are what I use most often, and they're perfect for serving as a side with a ton of recipes. When it comes to making specific rice dishes like risotto or paella, you need to use the correct rice, usually clearly labelled on the box.

Store rice in an airtight container and it will last for ages. Short on time? There's no shame in cracking out the microwave rice.

Noodles
Egg noodles – rice noodles – udon noodles
Noodles are speedy to cook. Just like pasta, certain noodles will work best with specific dishes but subbing one type in for another works just fine too.

Pulses & beans
Lentils – cannellini beans – butter beans – chickpeas – kidney beans
Beans count towards your five-a-day and are a great source of fibre. I use them a lot for cooking big, hearty meals, but they also work a treat as an added protein kick in lunch salads.

Canned tomatoes & tomato purée
One word of advice here: try to buy the best quality you can. It makes a difference.

Oils & butter

Butter – olive oil – extra virgin olive oil – vegetable/groundnut oil – toasted sesame oil

Butter is good on your toast, for cooking and baking. Olive oil is a great all-rounder for cooking. Extra virgin olive oil is perfect for dressings. You can use it for cooking, but not at a super high heat or it will burn. And don't store it in direct sunlight or it can go rancid. Vegetable oil and groundnut oil are good for frying at a high temperature. They have a fairly neutral flavour, which is why I use them for curries and stir-fries. Toasted sesame oil is a great add-on to home-cooked Chinese, Korean, Japanese and Thai recipes. Incredibly fragrant, it's perfect to add to sauces or at the end of a recipe for added flavour. Don't use it for frying though; it has a low smoking point, so will burn easily and taste off.

Vinegar

Balsamic – rice wine – red – white

Balsamic vinegar is great for dressings and serving with all things Italian. Rice wine vinegar works a treat in Chinese-style recipes. Red and white wine vinegars are super versatile and inexpensive and can be used for cooking, in dressings and in sauces.

Stock cubes

A very affordable way to add flavour, and 99 per cent of the time just as good as fresh stock, unless specified.

Spices

Garam masala - chilli powder (hot or mild, depending how you like it) – chilli flakes – ground cumin – ground coriander – smoked paprika – ground turmeric – curry powder (mild, medium or hot, whichever you prefer) – ground cinnamon or cinnamon sticks – black pepper

It's well worth having a good selection of spices at home. These are the ones you'll do well having to hand for the recipes in this book and beyond.

Dried herbs

Dried oregano – bay leaf – oregano – rosemary – thyme

I use a lot of fresh herbs, but dried herbs are great to have on standby – they don't cost much and will last much longer.

Frozen fruit & veg

Great value-for-money frozen fruit and vegetables are handy for the days you don't have time get to the shops. That way you can still whip up a nutritious meal with what you have at home. Frozen berries are perfect to chuck in a smoothie or to use as a porridge topper, like in my Cherry Bakewell porridge (see page 21) and can often be bought in a mixed bag for next to nothing.

Other basics I like to have handy

Fish sauce – soy sauce (light and dark) – chilli sauce – flour (plain, self-raising and cornflour) – honey – sugar (caster or granulated and a soft brown sugar) – oats – couscous – eggs – milk – Greek yoghurt – bread – onions – garlic

Kit list

You don't need a professional kitchen set-up at home to make delicious food from scratch. However, it is worth investing in some basics to allow you to cook a wide variety of food with ease. These are the bits and bobs I always think it's useful to have...

Large non-stick, ovenproof frying pan
The pan I use most often and the most versatile in my kitchen.

Casserole pan
Can be used on the hob and in the oven, so a great all-rounder and perfect for feeding a crowd.

Small non-stick frying pan
Does what it says on the tin. Try my Pesto baked eggs (see page 31)!

Non-stick saucepans, large & small
Another bit of everyday kit that will get well used from breakfast right through to dinner.

Griddle pan
This is a great way to give food a chargrilled smoky flavour and those classic bar marks. Perfect for meat and fish, and even toasts like bruschetta.

Deep-sided roasting tin
Just the thing to roast a chicken, like my Honey & harissa spatchcock chicken (see page 140).

Ovenproof dish
Great for lasagne, including my vegetarian one (see page 62)!

Baking tray
This can be used for roasting chicken breasts or making my Roast vegetable, pesto & mozzarella puff pastry tart (see page 71), baking and everything in between.

Chopping boards
It's always good to have a few of these. Plastic ones are great for prepping meat as you can chuck them straight in the dishwasher when you're done. Wooden ones work a treat for chopping veg.

Chef's knife
It's worth investing in a good-quality chef's knife. One will do if you're just starting out – you don't need to start with a full set. In my opinion the sharper the knife, the easier it is to chop and prep, making it all the more enjoyable (and quick!). Keep it sharp and look after it. Wash by hand in soapy water, then dry with a tea towel.

Mini food processor
This is a great investment; it isn't expensive and can be tucked away nicely. It's ace for making pestos, whizzing up breadcrumbs or making sauces like my peri peri or romesco (see pages 109 and 171).

Must-have utensils
- Wooden spoons
- Kitchen scissors
- Cheese grater
- Zester
- Rolling pin
- Tongs
- Fish slice
- Spatula

Chapters

Breakfast, brunch and lunch. Start the day right!

They say breakfast is the most important meal of the day, so I've got everything you need to start the day right – personally, that's got to be porridge, but there are loads of ideas for a lazy weekend brunch here, like my Sausage & egg breakfast tacos (see page 24). If you're whipping up lunch for friends, try the Tandoor-style salmon wraps and Chimichurri steak sarnie (see pages 50 and 34). Delicious!

Family favourites. Winning weeknight dinners.

You can't go wrong with the classics. There's something nostalgic and comforting about Sausage & mash with homemade onion gravy (see page 83) or a lovely bubbling hot lasagne (see page 62), piping hot and fresh out of the oven. These will fast become your go-to weeknight dinners, and you'll definitely be back for seconds.

Fakeaways. Recreating your favourite takeaways at home.

If you're anything like me, you love a good takeaway. But they can get expensive and you never quite know what's gone into them. So why not satisfy your cravings at home any night of the week with everything from the ultimate curry night to a kebab and anything in between. If you've got a bit of time, try your hand at a classic Chicken tikka masala (see page 98), or for something you can have on the table quicker than ordering a takeaway, my Drunken noodles are the answer (see page 102).

One pan. For people who hate washing up.

Ditch the washing up and dive into my one-pan wonders. You can pack so much flavour into a one-pan with very little effort. All of the flavour with none of the fuss – that's what we like. Between you and me, leftovers from my Arrabbiata sausage traybake (see page 146) make the best sausage sarnie ever the next day. It's almost worth making just for that!

Feeding a crowd. Feasting with family and friends.

I keep it simple when I've got company so I can spend more time with my mates and less time in the kitchen. You can have my Chilli prawn linguine on the table in 15 minutes (see page 173), or wow your friends with my Baked sea bass in black bean sauce (see page 168). It sounds fancy and tastes even fancier, but it's dead easy, proper dinner party stuff with a glass (or two) of wine.

Something sweet. The finishing touch.

There's always room for something sweet and there's nowt better than a freshly baked chocolate chip cookie from the oven (see page 200). Crispy on the edge with a melty, soft, chewy middle. As well as something to go with a cuppa, I've got a few dead easy puds, spot on after a dinner with family and friends.

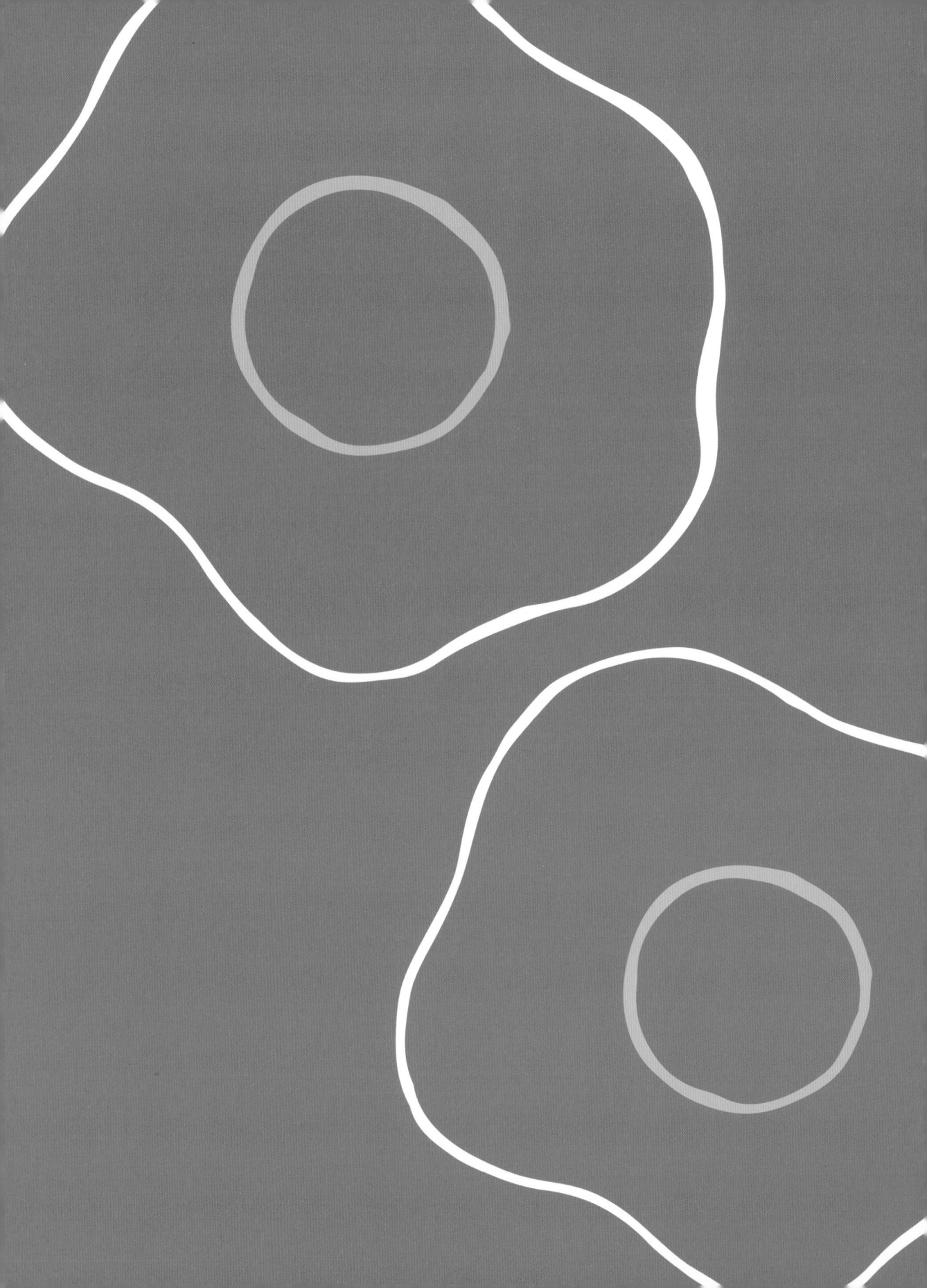

CHAPTER 1

Brunch

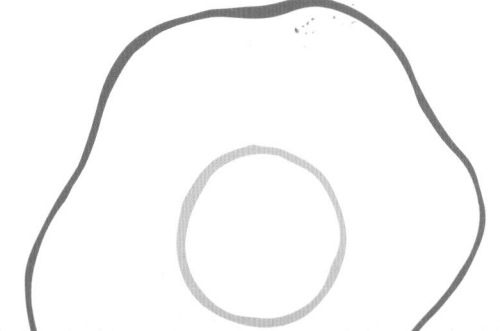

Porridge 3 Ways

I love porridge – I have it for breakfast most mornings! It's really filling and satisfying to eat. The key to a super creamy porridge is to keep stirring as it cooks, a bit like making a risotto. Here are a few of my favourite flavours to keep it interesting.

/ Simple Porridge

Serves 2 / 5 minutes

100g oats
600ml water or milk of your
　choice

This is to make 2 portions. If you are cooking for a crowd simply multiply the amounts by however many people you need to feed.

1. Put the oats into a saucepan with the water or milk.

2. Bring to the boil, then simmer for 4–5 minutes, stirring constantly until it reaches your desired consistency. There's no right or wrong here – it all comes down to personal preference. If you want it thicker, keep it cooking; if you want it looser, add a splash more water or milk.

/ Fresh Fig & Honey Porridge

Serves 2 / 6 minutes

100g oats
600ml water or milk of your
　choice
2 fresh figs, cut into quarters
2 tbsp honey
2 tbsp crushed walnuts

It doesn't get any easier than this! Sometimes less is more. I love fresh figs and this is the perfect way to enjoy them in the morning with a drizzle of honey. Spot on! Oh, and there's no need to peel the figs before you get started.

1. Cook the porridge following the method above.

2. Top with the fresh figs, drizzle over the honey and top with the walnuts.

/ Spiced Poached Pear Porridge

Serves 2 / 6 minutes

100g oats
600ml water or milk of your
   choice
1 large pear, diced
100ml boiling water
1 tsp ground mixed spice or
   cinnamon
2 tbsp maple syrup or honey,
   plus extra to serve
2 tbsp plain yoghurt

A proper winter warmer! You can't beat this on a cold morning to set you up for the day. You can make a big batch and store it in an airtight container in the fridge to last a few days. It also makes a tasty topping for yoghurt and granola.

1. Cook the porridge following the method opposite.

2. Meanwhile, heat a small pan over a medium high heat. Add the pear, boiling water, mixed spice and maple syrup or honey. Cook for about 5 minutes until the pear begins to soften but holds its shape and most of the liquid has evaporated, leaving a sticky syrup. Stir now and again.

3. Serve the poached pear on top of the porridge with a dollop of yoghurt. Add a drizzle more maple syrup or honey for sweetness.

/ Cherry Bakewell Porridge

Serves 2 / 6 minutes

200g frozen cherries
100g oats
600ml almond milk
2 tsp almond or vanilla extract
2 heaped tbsp almond butter,
   plus extra to serve
2 tbsp honey, plus extra to
   serve
2 tbsp flaked almonds

Cherry and almond is a classic combo and it makes for a tasty breakfast. You can use any frozen berry for this or if cherries are in season, use them fresh and just pop out the stones before you get cooking. I like to use almond milk rather than regular milk or water for the porridge here for an extra nutty flavour.

1. Put the cherries in a bowl and pour over a splash of boiling water to defrost them; it will take a few minutes. Drain off the water. Keep 6 cherries aside for later then gently mash the rest of the cherries in the bowl with a fork.

2. Meanwhile, cook the porridge following the method opposite, adding the almond extract as it cooks. When the porridge is cooked, stir in the mashed cherries, with any juice from the bowl, and the almond butter and honey.

3. Top with the remaining cherries and flaked almonds with a drizzle more honey and almond butter to serve.

Eggy Bread with Lemon Ricotta & Blueberries

Serves 2 / 10 minutes

4 tbsp ricotta
1 lemon
2 eggs
1 tsp sugar, white or brown
1 tbsp butter
2 thick slices of slightly stale
   white bread

To serve
160g blueberries
2 tbsp honey

This is a fantastic way to use bread that's starting to go stale. I like to use a good-quality white loaf cut into nice thick 1.5cm slices. The sweet and savoury mix of ricotta and honey is a winner. Why not give it a go with some added fresh strawberries in the summer?

1. Put the ricotta into a small bowl. Use a zester or fine grater to remove the lemon zest and add to the ricotta. Mix together with a little squeeze of lemon juice, then set aside.

2. Crack the eggs into a small bowl, add the sugar and lightly whisk with a fork until the whites and yolks are combined.

3. Heat the butter in a non-stick frying pan over a medium heat until the butter begins to foam.

4. While the pan is heating, dip each slice of bread into the egg mixture one at a time. Hold down for a couple of seconds on each side to soak up the egg.

5. Lift the bread from the bowl, allowing any excess liquid to drip off.

6. Fry the bread in the butter for about 2 minutes on each side or until golden.

7. Put each slice on to a serving plate. Spread over a dollop of lemon ricotta, then scatter over the blueberries and drizzle with honey.

Sausage & Egg Breakfast Tacos

Serves 2 / 15 minutes

1 avocado
1 tbsp olive oil
4 sausages, roughly chopped
1 small onion, finely chopped
1 red or green chilli, chopped
  and deseeded if you prefer
  a milder taste
2 tsp fajita mix or Cajun
  spice mix
1 lime
1 small bunch of coriander,
  chopped
1 tbsp butter
2 eggs, lightly beaten with
  a fork
4 small soft tortillas
Hot or sweet chilli sauce
Salt and pepper

This nice and spicy spin on sausage and eggs is perfect for a lazy weekend breakfast or brunch. If you're anything like me and love a bit of spice in the morning, leave the seeds in the chilli for more of a kick.

1. Remove the flesh from the avocado. Add it to a bowl with a pinch of salt and pepper, crush with a fork and set aside.

2. Heat the olive oil in a large non-stick frying pan over a medium–high heat.

3. Add the sausage meat, onion and half the chilli and fry for 5–7 minutes or until golden and caramelised.

4. Stir in the fajita mix with a splash of water, reduce the heat and cook for 2 minutes until most of the water has evaporated. Add a squeeze of lime juice, stir in most of the coriander and remove from the heat.

5. While the sausage is cooking, add the butter to a small saucepan over a medium heat. Add the eggs, season and cook for about 2 minutes, stirring gently, until scrambled and just cooked.

6. Heat the tacos in the microwave for 10 seconds.

7. Assemble the tacos. Put 2 tacos on to each serving plate. Spread with avocado, top with the sausage mixture, then add the egg. Scatter over the remaining chopped chilli and coriander. Drizzle with chilli sauce and serve.

Cheesy Bacon Potato Cake with Crispy Fried Egg

Serves 2 / 30 minutes

Approx. 500g mashed potato
100g Cheddar cheese
3 tbsp olive oil
4 slices of bacon, roughly
   chopped
1 tbsp butter
1 large leek, finely sliced
2 eggs
Brown sauce
Salt and pepper

This is the perfect way to use up leftover mashed potato. You don't need to be exact with the amount, and if you haven't got leftover mash, you can always boil up some potatoes and make a fresh batch. I love this with some good old brown sauce, but you can use whatever takes your fancy, or raid the fridge. Leave out the bacon if you want to go veggie.

1. Put the mashed potato into a mixing bowl, then grate in the cheese.

2. Add 1 tbsp of oil to a medium non-stick frying pan over a medium heat. Fry the bacon for 3–5 minutes until crisp, then add it to the mash and cheese, leaving the bacon fat in the pan.

3. Add the leek to the pan. Season and cook in the bacon fat for 5–8 minutes until softened. Remove from the heat, then add to the potatoes and bacon and give it a good mix together.

4. Put the pan back on the heat with 1 tbsp of oil and the butter. When the butter has melted and begins to sizzle, add the potato mixture and press down firmly with a spatula, spreading it across the pan to form the cake. Fry for 5–6 minutes until golden on the base

5. Slide on to a plate. Place another plate on top and flip over. Then slide it back into the pan and cook for a further 5 minutes or until golden.

6. Meanwhile, heat 1 tbsp of oil in a frying pan over a medium heat. Fry the eggs for about 2 minutes until the whites are just set and the yolks are still soft.

7. Cut the potato cake into wedges, serve with a fried egg and any sauce you've got in the fridge.

Garlic Mushrooms on Toast with Melting Taleggio Cheese

Serves 4 / 12 minutes

25g butter, plus extra for
buttering the bread
2 garlic cloves, chopped
600g chestnut mushrooms,
sliced
8 sprigs of thyme, leaves
picked
4 slices of sourdough
200g Taleggio cheese, cut into
5mm slices
Drizzle of extra virgin olive oil
Salt and pepper

These mushrooms cooked in butter with garlic and thyme make for the ultimate toast topper! Garlic mushrooms might be old school but they still deliver every time. Taleggio is a semi-soft Italian cheese; if you can't get hold of it, some Brie or even grated Cheddar will do the job and take this classic to a whole new level.

1. Preheat the grill setting on the oven to high.

2. Melt the butter in a large non-stick frying pan over a high heat.

3. Fry the garlic for 30 seconds, then add the mushrooms and thyme and season with salt and pepper. Cook for 5–8 minutes until all of the liquid has evaporated from the mushrooms.

4. Meanwhile, toast and butter the bread, then place on a baking tray.

5. When the mushrooms are cooked, divide them between the toast and top each with cheese.

6. Pop under the grill until the cheese is just melted.

7. Serve with black pepper and a drizzle of extra virgin olive oil.

Courgette Fritters with Poached Eggs

Serves 2 / 20 minutes, *plus 15 minutes resting*

2 courgettes, grated
  (approx. 500g)
1 small red onion, finely diced
1 handful of fresh peas *(or frozen peas, defrosted)*
1 garlic clove, grated or crushed
1 small bunch of flat-leaf parsley or mint, finely chopped
Zest of 1 lemon *(save the juice to serve)*
100g feta cheese, crumbled
3 eggs, 1 lightly beaten
Pinch of chilli flakes *(optional)*
100g self-raising flour
2 tbsp olive oil
1 tbsp malt or white wine vinegar
Salt and pepper

This dish might sound a bit fancy, but it's dead easy to make. A couple of top tips here: squeeze as much water from the courgettes as possible. There's nowt worse than a soggy fritter! Also, don't overcook your eggs. You want a nice runny, rich egg yolk to ooze all over the crispy fritters.

1. Place the grated courgettes and chopped onion into a large mixing bowl. Season with salt, mix and set aside for 15 minutes to allow the salt to draw out any moisture.

2. Pour out any liquid from the bowl. Then, using both hands, squeeze out any excess liquid over the sink. Return the courgettes to the bowl and pat dry with kitchen paper.

3. Add the peas, garlic, parsley, lemon zest, feta, beaten egg and chilli, if using. Mix together, then stir in the flour to form a thick, sticky batter, adding a touch more flour if it's very loose.

4. Divide the batter into 6 balls.

5. Heat the olive oil in a large non-stick frying pan over a medium heat. Add the fritter balls to the pan, then gently flatten with the back of the spoon until 1cm thick.

6. Fry for 2–3 minutes on each side until golden. You may need to do this in 2 batches.

7. Meanwhile, bring a small saucepan of water to a simmer with the vinegar. Gently crack in the eggs. Poach for 2–3 minutes until the whites are set, then remove with a slotted spoon.

8. Serve 3 fritters per person. Top with a poached egg, a squeeze of lemon juice and twist of pepper.

Pesto Baked Eggs

Serves 1 / 20 minutes

1 tbsp extra virgin olive oil, plus
  extra to serve
1 garlic clove, sliced
400g can cherry tomatoes
3 tbsp basil pesto
2 eggs
Salt and pepper

Bread, to serve

This tasty little number goes to show you can make a belter of a brunch with a few simple storecupboard ingredients in no time. If you have any fresh herbs lying around like basil or parsley, throw them on at the end. If you can't get any canned cherry tomatoes, a can of chopped tomatoes works just as well.

1. Heat the oil in a small frying pan over a medium–high heat.

2. Fry the garlic for 30 seconds, then stir in the tomatoes and 2 tbsp of the pesto and season with salt and pepper.

3. Bring to the boil, then reduce the heat to medium, cover loosely and simmer for 8–10 minutes until you have a fairly thick sauce.

4. Use a spoon to make 2 wells in the tomatoes. Crack an egg into each well, cover and cook for about 5 minutes or until the whites are set and the yolks are still soft.

5. Take off the heat, spoon over the remaining pesto and drizzle with a little more oil. Serve with bread to dip in the egg yolk and sauce.

Spicy Bacon & Egg Breakfast Bagels

Makes 2 / 10 minutes

2 bagels
2 tbsp chilli jam
1 avocado, flesh removed
  and crushed
1 tbsp olive oil
4 rashers of bacon
2 eggs
Salt and pepper

What's not to love about a fancy spin on a bacon sarnie with a spicy kick – perfect for a lazy Sunday morning!

1. Slice the bagels in half. Spread the insides with chilli jam, then top the base with the crushed avocado and season with salt and pepper.

2. Heat the oil in a large non-stick frying pan over a medium–high heat. Fry the bacon for 2–3 minutes on each side until cooked to your liking.

3. Add the cooked bacon to the base of each bagel on top of the avocado.

4. Return the pan to the heat and gently crack in the eggs. Fry for about 2 minutes or until the whites are set and the yolks are still runny.

5. Place the fried eggs on to the bacon, top with the bagel lids and serve.

Harissa Lamb
Sausage Rolls

Makes 4 large or 12 mini sausage rolls / 50 minutes, *plus cooling time*

1 tbsp vegetable oil
1 onion, finely chopped
3 garlic cloves, chopped
2 tbsp harissa paste
400g lamb mince
70g fresh breadcrumbs
75g dried apricots, chopped
1 small bunch of mint, finely
　chopped
1 small bunch of flat-leaf
　parsley, finely copped
320g ready-roll puff pastry
1 egg, beaten
Pinch of ground cinnamon
Salt and pepper

Tzatziki (see page 114), to serve

What can I say, I'm from the northeast, so a sausage roll had to make an appearance somewhere in this book. This is a spicy Middle Eastern-inspired spin on the classic that I created for M&S Food. It's not spicy hot, just mild and aromatic with a touch of sweetness. It's great fresh and warm straight from the oven, but just as good cold as a killer addition to a picnic. Simply store in the fridge in an airtight container for up to 2 days.

1. Preheat the oven to 220°C/200°C fan.

2. Heat the vegetable oil in a saucepan over a medium heat, add the onion and garlic and cook for 8 minutes until softened.

3. Add the harissa paste and cook for a further 4 minutes, season with salt and pepper, then allow to cool.

4. Stir in the lamb, breadcrumbs, apricots and herbs until well combined.

5. Lay the pastry on a flat surface and cut in half lengthways so you have two long, thin rectangles.

6. Split the filling in half and spread each portion lengthways along the top third of each piece of pastry.

7. Fold the pastry over to cover the filling and crimp the edge with a fork to seal.

8. Brush all over with the beaten egg, sprinkle with the cinnamon and a pinch of salt.

9. Cut each piece in half to give you 4 sausage rolls, then transfer to a baking tray.

10. Bake for about 25 minutes until golden and the lamb is cooked though with no pink remaining. Serve with tzatziki.

Chimichurri Steak Sarnie

Serves 2 / 15 minutes

1 large sirloin steak
1 ciabatta loaf
1 tbsp olive oil
Approx. 100g watercress
Salt and pepper

For the sauce

1 small bunch of flat-leaf
  parsley, finely chopped
1 small bunch of coriander,
  finely chopped
3 tbsp red wine vinegar
4 tbsp extra virgin olive oil
1 tsp dried oregano
1 red chilli, finely chopped
1 garlic clove, grated or
  crushed

A nice big, warm ciabatta filled with juicy steak and fresh, zingy sauce; I mean come on! I'm hungry just thinking about it. I first made this while filming with M&S Food in my home county of Northumberland and it's got to be up there as one of the best sandwiches ever. My top tip here is to slice the meat against the grain, this will give you the most tender bite.

1. Remove the steak from the fridge 30 minutes before cooking.

2. Preheat the oven to 200°C/180°C fan.

3. Bake the ciabatta for 8–10 minutes until just crisp

4. In a small bowl, mix the herbs, red wine vinegar, oil, oregano, chilli and garlic together to make the sauce.

5. Drizzle the steak with 1 tbsp olive oil and season all over with salt and pepper.

6. Heat a non-stick frying pan or griddle pan over a very high heat.

7. For a medium steak, fry it for about 2 minutes on each side. If you prefer your steak rare, fry for about 90 seconds per side, or for well done, 3 minutes per side.

8. Remove the steak from the heat and place it on a plate to rest for 5 minutes before slicing into thin strips. Season it again with salt.

9. Cut the ciabatta open and drizzle each side with some of the sauce. Add the watercress and then top with the sliced steak. Pour over any remaining sauce and serve.

Lime & Coriander Prawn Tostadas

Serves 4 / 10–15 minutes

Approx. 360g raw king prawns
2 tbsp olive oil
2 avocados
2 limes, 1 cut into wedges
8 small tortillas
Chilli sauce

For the marinade

2 tbsp lime juice
2 garlic cloves, grated
½ small bunch of coriander,
  finely chopped
1 tsp ground cumin

For the slaw

¼ red cabbage, finely sliced
1 large carrot, grated
4 spring onions, chopped
1 red chilli, finely chopped
  and deseeded if you prefer
  a milder taste
Juice of ½ lime
1 tsp caster sugar
1 tbsp extra virgin olive oil
½ small bunch of coriander,
  finely chopped
Salt and pepper

A tostada is a Mexican dish made with a toasted or fried tortilla, so make sure to get them nice and crispy in a super hot frying pan. Crispy tortillas, creamy avo, crunchy slaw, juicy prawns in a lime and coriander marinade with chilli sauce – what's not to like? !

1. Mix all the slaw ingredients together in a bowl, season and set aside.

2. In a bowl, mix the prawns together with half the oil and all the marinade ingredients, saving half of the coriander to use in the slaw. Set aside for 5 minutes.

3. Mash the flesh of the avocados in a small bowl with a squeeze of lime juice, season and set aside.

4. Heat a dry large non-stick frying pan over a high heat. Toast the tortillas for about 30 seconds on each side until lightly golden and crisp. Remove to a plate and cover with a clean tea towel or foil to keep warm.

5. Put the pan back over the heat and add 1 tbsp olive oil. Stir-fry the prawns for 2–3 minutes until they are pink, then remove from the heat. Add the remaining coriander.

6. Spread the avocado over the toasted tortillas. Top with the slaw and prawns. Drizzle with chilli sauce. Serve with a wedge of lime to squeeze over the top.

Jalapeño Chilli Cheese Toastie

Makes 1 / 5–10 minutes

Approx. 25g butter
2 slices of sourdough bread
1 tbsp chilli jam
2 tbsp sliced jalapeños from
 a jar
50g Cheddar cheese, grated
1 spring onion, finely chopped
1 tbsp olive oil

There's something magic about an oozy cheese toastie – you just can't beat it! This is a bit fancier than what I used to whip up in our old toastie maker growing up, but just as easy. The sweet and salty combo of cheese and chilli jam is a match made in heaven, with a kick of spice from the jalapeños.

1. Butter the outside of each slice of bread.

2. With the butter-side down, spread the inside of one slice with the chilli jam and then top with a few jalapeños, the cheese and spring onion.

3. Put the other slice on top, butter-side up, and gently press it down.

4. Heat the oil in a large non-stick frying pan on a medium heat.

5. Fry the sandwich for 2–3 minutes until the base is golden. Press it down with the back of a spatula, then flip over and cook for a further 2–3 minutes until golden on the other side.

Harissa Beans with Honey-Glazed Halloumi

Serves 2 / 20 minutes

1 tbsp olive oil
2 garlic cloves, chopped
1 red pepper, chopped
1 tbsp harissa paste
400g can mixed beans, drained
400g can chopped tomatoes
½ tsp ground cinnamon
1 tsp dried oregano
100g halloumi cheese, cut into thin slices
2 tbsp honey
2 slices of bread, white or brown, depending on what you prefer
Butter, for the toast
Salt and pepper

This recipe will take your beans on toast game to another level. Spicy beans with salty, sweet and sticky honey-glazed halloumi. Once you've mastered the halloumi, you'll be eating it with everything! It works well with my Roast cauliflower kebabs (see page 106), Spiced veggie pilaf (see page 136) and Courgette fritters (see page 28).

1. Heat the olive oil in a large saucepan over a medium heat.

2. Fry the garlic and pepper with a pinch of salt for 5 minutes until softened.

3. Add the harissa, cook for 30 seconds, then add the beans, tomatoes, cinnamon and oregano. Season with salt and pepper and cook over a medium–high heat for 10–15 minutes until thickened.

4. Meanwhile, heat a small frying pan over a medium heat with no oil. Add the sliced halloumi and fry for 1 minute on each side until golden. Drizzle over the honey, let it bubble for 30 seconds and turn off the heat.

5. Toast and butter the bread, then pile on the beans and top with the honey-glazed halloumi.

Blackened Cajun Salmon with Homemade Salsa

Serves 2 / 10 minutes

2 salmon fillets
1 tbsp olive oil, plus extra
  for drizzling
4 tbsp Cajun spice mix

Rice, to serve (optional)

For the salsa
1 avocado, diced
Handful of cherry tomatoes,
  quartered
165g can sweetcorn, drained
1 small bunch of coriander,
  chopped
Zest and juice of 1 lime
2 tbsp olive oil
1 red or green chilli, deseeded
  and chopped (optional)
Salt and pepper

This recipe is a quick and easy way to give salmon a spicy kick, not to mention a great way to cook it. You get an incredibly crispy edge with a soft, flaking delicate centre. When it comes to the salsa, make it your own and tweak the flavour just how you like it. This dish works a treat served with rice. Try wholegrain or even a spicy pre-cooked pouch.

1. Mix all the salsa ingredients together in a bowl with a pinch of salt and pepper, then set aside.

2. Drizzle each salmon fillet in oil.

3. Spread the Cajun spice mix on a plate. Pop the salmon on top and coat it evenly on each side.

4. Heat 1 tbsp olive oil in a non-stick frying pan over a medium–high heat.

5. Fry the salmon for 2 minutes on each side until you have a blackened crust, really allowing it to char. Then cook the edges for 30 seconds to crisp up. Remove from the heat.

6. Serve with the salsa and rice, if using.

Chargrilled Peach & Asparagus Salad with Goat's Cheese

Serves 2 as a main or 4 as a side / 10–15 minutes

1 small bunch of mint leaves, half chopped and half left whole
4 tbsp extra virgin olive oil
Zest of 1 lemon, juice of half
4 tsp honey, plus extra for drizzling
2 peaches, cut into wedges
250g asparagus, woody ends removed
100g rocket
150g goat's cheese
Salt and pepper

Asparagus is one of the British ingredients I get most excited about. I only eat it in season when it's at its best. Charring it like this gives a lovely nutty flavour, which works a treat with the sweet peach and salty goat's cheese!

1. To make the dressing, mix together the chopped mint leaves, 3 tbsp extra virgin olive oil, the zest and juice of half the lemon and 1 tsp of the honey in a bowl with a pinch of salt and pepper. Adjust the flavour to your own taste. Set aside.

2. Put the peaches and asparagus into a bowl, drizzle with 1 tbsp oil, season and toss together.

3. Heat a griddle pan until smoking hot. Griddle the asparagus for about 3 minutes until charred, turning now and again. Remove from the pan and set aside on a plate.

4. Griddle the peaches for 1 minute on each side or until golden and slightly charred. Drizzle over the remaining 3 tsp honey and let it bubble away for 30 seconds, then remove from the pan.

5. Place the rocket on a serving plate with the whole mint leaves, asparagus and peaches. Drizzle with half the dressing and toss together. Sprinkle over the remaining lemon zest, then crumble in the goat's cheese. Serve with a drizzle more dressing and honey.

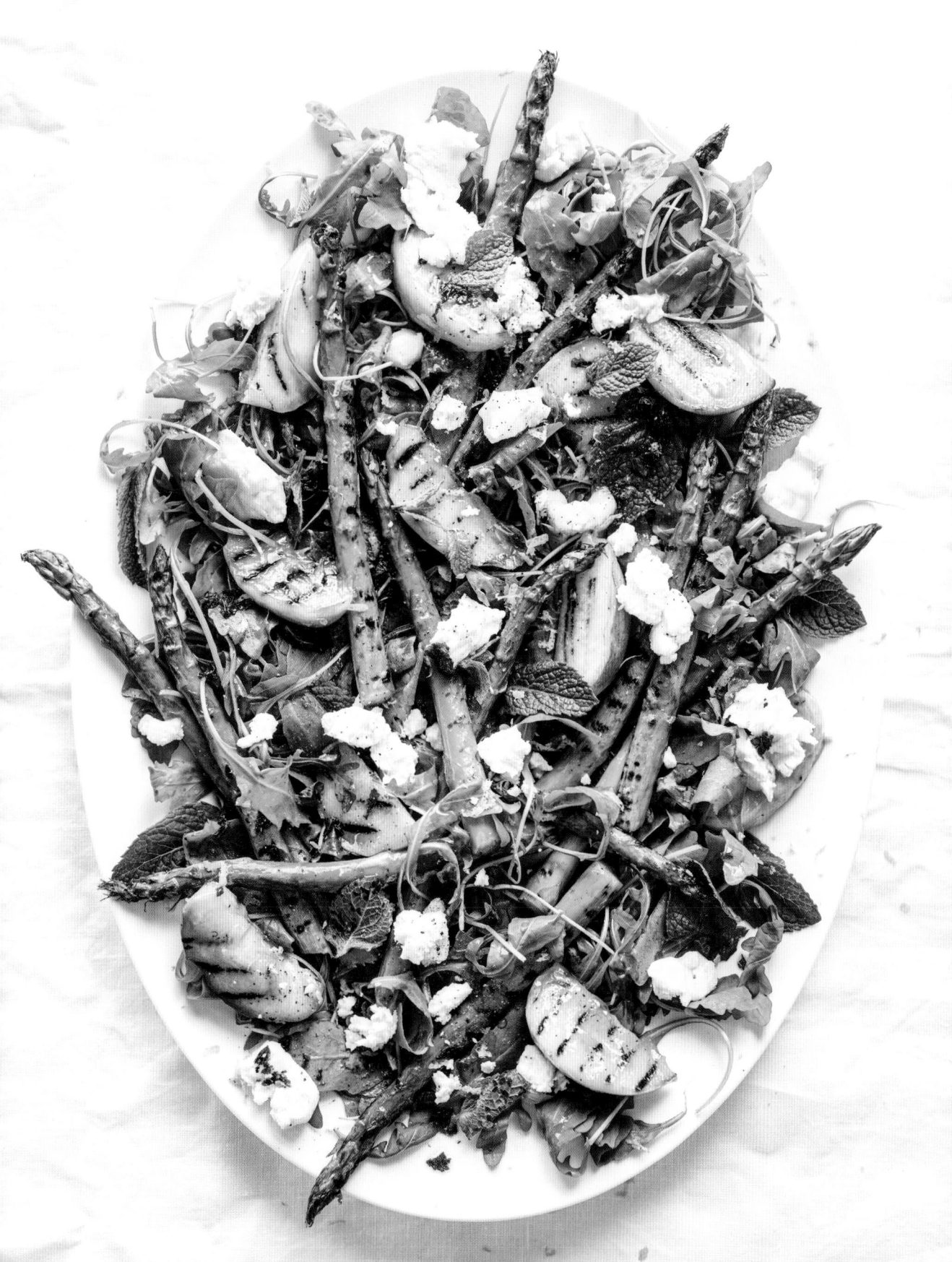

Easy Pea Soup
with Crispy Croutons

Serves 4 / 20 minutes

4 slices of white bread, cut in
to 2cm cubes
1 tbsp olive oil
1 tbsp butter
1 large onion, chopped
2 garlic cloves, chopped
600g frozen peas, defrosted
100g watercress
600ml vegetable stock
4 tbsp crème fraîche
(optional)
Salt and pepper

This is a really handy recipe to have up your sleeve for lunch, and makes a dead easy starter if you've got people coming over. Feeling fancy? To make it a bit 'posher' for fussy dinner guests, you can stir in 1 tbsp crème fraîche at the end.

1. Preheat the oven to 200°C/180°C fan.

2. Put the bread on a baking tray, drizzle with the olive oil, season and toss together.

3. Bake for about 10 minutes or until golden and crispy.

4. Meanwhile, heat the butter in a saucepan over a medium heat. Add the onion and garlic, season and fry for 5–8 minutes until softened, stirring now and again.

5. Add the peas and watercress, then pour in the stock and simmer for 5 minutes.

6. Remove from the heat and blitz until smooth with a hand blender; add a splash of boiling water if you want a thinner soup.

7. Serve with the crispy croutons and crème fraîche.

Hot-Smoked Salmon & Potato Salad with Crème Fraîche Dressing

Serves 4 / 20–25 minutes

1kg new potatoes, halved
300–400g asparagus
4 tbsp crème fraîche
1 tbsp horseradish sauce
Zest and juice of 1 lemon
2 tbsp extra virgin olive oil
1 small bunch of dill, finely chopped
350g hot-smoked salmon
Salt and pepper

This is a substantial warm salad that makes the most of some lovely British ingredients. It's worth getting Jersey Royals when they are in season. When it comes to the dressing, have a taste and make it your own by adding more horseradish and lemon.

1. Cook the potatoes for 15–20 minutes in a large pan of boiling salted water until tender. Drain and set aside.

2. While the potatoes are cooking, discard the woody ends of the asparagus – you'll feel a natural snapping point close to the base.

3. In a small bowl, mix together the crème fraîche and horseradish with the zest of the lemon and 2 tbsp of its juice. Season to taste.

4. Heat 1 tbsp of oil a large non-stick frying pan over a medium–high heat. Add the asparagus and cook for 2–3 minutes, turning now and again until slightly charred and golden. Remove from the heat.

5. Put the potatoes and asparagus into a large bowl. Drizzle with the remaining 1 tbsp of oil and scatter over the dill, season with salt and pepper, then add half the dressing and gently toss together.

6. Divide among 4 serving plates, then flake over the salmon and drizzle with more dressing.

7. Serve with a quick squeeze of lemon juice.

Bang Bang Chicken Salad

Serves 2 / 30 minutes

2 skinless chicken breasts or
   leftover cooked chicken
100ml water
2 limes
5 tbsp olive oil
Salt and pepper

For the salad
1 baby gem lettuce, finely
   shredded
½ cucumber, finely diced
1 large carrot, grated
2 spring onions, finely sliced
75g sugar snap peas, finely
   sliced
1 small bunch of coriander,
   finely chopped

For the dressing
4 tbsp smooth peanut butter
2 tbsp sweet chilli or sriracha
   sauce

For the garnish
Handful of salted peanuts,
   crushed
1 red chilli, chopped *(optional)*

If you are looking for a salad that's big on flavour, this is it. The peanut dressing is so easy to make and packs a real punch. If you want to make this into a bigger meal, chuck some cooked egg noodles into the salad.

1. Preheat the oven to 200°C/180°C fan.

2. Put the raw chicken in a baking tray and season with salt and pepper. Add the water to the tray. Bake for about 25 minutes until the chicken is cooked with no pink remaining; to check, cut into the middle of one of the chicken breasts. Roughly shred the chicken using 2 forks.

3. While the chicken is cooking, prepare the salad. Add all the ingredients to a large bowl with the juice of ½ lime and 1 tbsp olive oil, toss together and set aside.

4. For the dressing, mix together the peanut butter and chilli sauce with the zest and juice of ½ lime, 4 tbsp olive oil and a pinch of salt until smooth. Adjust the flavour to your taste by adding more lime, chilli, oil or peanut butter.

5. Divide the salad between the serving plates. Top with the shredded chicken, then drizzle over the peanut dressing. Scatter with peanuts and chopped chilli and squeeze over more lime juice to serve.

Tandoor-Style Salmon Wraps

Serves 2 / 25 minutes, *plus 30 minutes–2 hours marinating*

2 salmon fillets
2 naans

For the salad
2 tomatoes, finely diced
1 small red onion, finely sliced
1 small bunch of coriander,
 finely chopped
Pinch of salt

For the sauce
2 tbs Greek yoghurt
2 tsp mint sauce

For the marinade
2 tbsp Greek yoghurt
1 heaped tsp medium
 curry powder
Juice of ¼ lemon
1 tsp honey
Pinch of salt

This reminds me of one of the most memorable dishes I've ever eaten. Before I began working with Atul Kochhar, he invited me down to his restaurant in London to meet. I had a few drinks in the bar, then we had a chat. Slightly tipsy, he sent me on my way with some food. I went and sat in Mayfair and tucked into the most incredible and memorable takeout ever: a warm naan full of sauce and meat from the tandoor. I'll never forget that moment or what Atul has done for me since.

1. Mix the marinade ingredients together in a bowl. Add the salmon and coat in the marinade. Transfer to the fridge for 30 minutes–2 hours to marinate.

2. For the salad, simply mix the tomatoes, onion and coriander together with the salt,

3. For the sauce, mix together the yoghurt and mint sauce.

4. Preheat the oven to 220°C/200°C fan.

5. Lay the salmon on a baking tray and cover with any excess marinade. Bake for 10–12 minutes until slightly golden brown.

6. Warm the breads according to the packet instructions.

7. Lay the warm breads on a board. Scatter with salad, flake over the cooked salmon, then drizzle over the yoghurt sauce. Finish with a squeeze more lemon juice.

8. Roll them up like a wrap or leave open to eat with a knife and fork.

Cheesy Chilli Leek & Pea Frittata

Serves 2 / **15–20 minutes**

1 tbsp butter
1 leek, finely sliced
1 red chilli, deseeded and
 chopped
150g frozen peas, defrosted
5 eggs, lightly beaten
75g Cheddar cheese, grated,
 or 75g goat's cheese,
 crumbled
Salt and pepper

A really simple, fresh recipe you can have on the table in just 20 minutes. Try swapping the peas for asparagus when it's in season – just chop it into bite-sized pieces. This dish is lovely with a handful of rocket or watercress on the side.

1. Preheat the oven to 200°C/180°C fan.

2. Melt the butter in a small ovenproof frying pan over a medium heat.

3. Fry the leek and chilli with salt and pepper for 5 minutes until softened, then add the peas.

4. Stir in the eggs and half the cheese. Cook on the hob for 1 minute, then scatter the remaining cheese on top and finish cooking in the oven for about 10 minutes until the eggs are set and the cheese is golden on top.

CHAPTER 2

Family Faves

Creamy Prawn Pasta with Ginger & Lime

Serves 4 / 10–15 minutes

400g fusilli
2 tbsp extra virgin olive oil
2 garlic cloves, sliced
2 courgettes, cut into half moons
300g raw prawns
2cm piece of fresh ginger, peeled and grated
1 tbsp tomato purée
4 tbsp crème fraîche
Zest and juice of 1 lime
1 tsp chilli flakes
Salt and pepper

On a family holiday in the Italian lakes in 2017, I discovered an amazing little restaurant serving this incredible seafood pasta using ginger and lime. It's not the sort of flavour combination you'd expect in Italian food, but it really works. Perfect in the summer with glass of wine. If you want to make this veggie, just leave out the prawns and chuck in an extra courgette. Simple.

1. Cook the pasta in a large pan of boiling salted water for 2 minutes less than the packet instructions. Drain, saving half a mug of the pasta cooking water, and set aside for now.

2. Meanwhile, heat the oil in a large non-stick frying pan over a medium heat.

3. Add the garlic, fry for 30 seconds and then add the courgettes. Season and stir-fry for a further 5 minutes.

4. Add the prawns, ginger and tomato purée. Cook for 1–2 minutes until the prawns are pink, stirring constantly.

5. Add half of the reserved pasta water, then turn down the heat and stir in the crème fraîche.

6. Add the drained pasta to the prawns, toss together and cook for another minute or so, adding more pasta cooking water if needed to loosen the sauce,

7. Add the lime zest and a little squeeze of its juice. Remove from the heat.

8. Serve with a pinch of chilli flakes, a drizzle of olive oil and a squeeze more lime juice.

Summer Salmon Lemon & Pea Farfalle

Serves 4 / 10–12 minutes

360–400g farfalle
1 tbsp olive oil
1 onion, finely chopped
1 garlic clove, grated or crushed
1 tsp fennel seeds
½ tsp chilli flakes
2 salmon fillets, cut into
  1cm cubes
5 tbsp crème fraîche
200g fresh peas
Zest and juice of 1 lemon
Salt and pepper

This is one of the recipes I developed for M&S Food – which we filmed for the telly next to Loch Linnhe in Scotland. There really is no better place to cook up a salmon storm, right next to where it was caught! Every time I make this it brings back good memories of all the crew getting stuck into it for lunch. It's also a fantastic way to make 2 fillets of salmon feed a family of 4, and I love the creamy sauce with the sweet peas.

1. Cook the pasta in a large pan of boiling salted water for 8–10 minutes until al dente (it should still have a bit of bite).

2. Meanwhile, in a large non-stick frying pan, heat the olive oil over a medium heat.

3. Add the onion, garlic, fennel seeds and chilli flakes and season with salt and pepper. Cook for 5 minutes until softened.

4. Turn up the heat, add the salmon and cook for another minute, allowing the fish to become slightly golden and caramelised.

5. Turn the heat down to low, add the crème fraîche to the pan with 5 tbsp of the pasta cooking water. Use a spoon to add this from the pasta as it's cooking, then stir together.

6. Add the peas and cook for a further 2 minutes

7. Drain the pasta, saving a little more of the pasta cooking water. Add the pasta to the sauce with the lemon zest and juice and toss everything together, adding a little more pasta water to loosen the sauce if needed.

Veggie Lasagne

Serves 4 / 1 hour 5 minutes

2 tbsp olive oil
2 onions, cut into 2cm chunks
1 aubergine, cut into 2cm chunks
2 peppers, cut into 2cm chunks
2 courgettes, cut into 2cm
   chunks
2 garlic cloves, grated or
   crushed
1 tbsp dried oregano
1 small bunch of basil, leaves
   and stalks roughly torn
   into pieces
1 tbsp balsamic vinegar
2 x 400g cans chopped
   tomatoes
250–300g lasagne sheets
150g Cheddar cheese, grated
Salt and pepper

For the sauce
60g butter
60g plain flour
1 garlic clove, grated
600ml semi-skimmed milk
Grating of ¼ nutmeg *(optional)*
20g Parmesan cheese, grated
   (optional)

To serve
Garlic baguette
Salad

A lasagne served up with a garlic baguette and salad is proper home cooking at its finest. I came up with this veggie version, which is a bit lighter but still gives you everything you want from a good lasagne – a rich, creamy garlic-infused sauce with a flavoursome filling.

1. Preheat the oven to 200°C/180°C fan.

2. Heat the olive oil in a very large saucepan or frying pan over a high heat. Fry the onion and aubergine with salt and pepper for 5 minutes until the onion takes on some colour and begins to turn light brown.

3. Add the peppers, courgette, garlic and oregano. Cook for a further 3–5 minutes until the veg begins to soften.

4. Add the basil, balsamic vinegar and chopped tomatoes. Fill your leftover chopped tomato cans with a splash of water in each can to rinse out all of the tomato, and chuck the water in the pan. Increase the heat to high, bring the filling to the boil, then reduce the heat and cover loosely. Simmer for 20–25 minutes until thick and rich. Stir occasionally.

5. While the veg is cooking, make the sauce. Melt the butter in a saucepan over a medium heat. Add the flour and garlic and cook for a couple of minutes, stirring regularly, to make a paste.

6. Gradually add the milk, stirring until the mixture is smooth.

7. Season with salt and pepper and add the nutmeg, if using. Simmer gently for 10 minutes or until it thickens (a consistency a bit like custard is what you're after). Stir in the Parmesan and remove from the heat.

8. Once the veg has had 20–25 minutes in the pan, check the seasoning. Then transfer half of it into an ovenproof dish.

9. Cover with lasagne sheets (if they don't fit exactly into the dish, you can snap them and put them together like a jigsaw), then spread over half the sauce. Repeat the process with the remaining veg, more pasta sheets and sauce like a layer cake.

10. Top with the grated cheese and bake for 30 minutes, or until the cheese on top is golden and the lasagne is bubbling away nicely.

11. Leave to cool for 10 minutes before serving with a garlic baguette and salad.

Roast Squash Risotto with Toasted Pine Nuts

Serves 4 / 30–35 minutes

100g pine nuts
2 butternut squash, peeled
  and cut into 2cm pieces
6 sprigs of fresh thyme
4 tbsp extra virgin olive oil, plus
  extra for drizzling
1.5 litres vegetable stock from
  a pouch or made with
  2 stock cubes
1 onion, finely chopped
2 garlic cloves, chopped
2 tsp dried oregano
400g risotto rice
40g unsalted butter
50g Parmesan cheese, grated
1 small bunch of basil,
  leaves picked
Salt and pepper

A risotto is actually really simple to make and using roast squash is just perfect in the autumn and winter on a cold night. If you want to make it extra indulgent, add extra butter and Parmesan at the end!

1. Preheat the oven to 220°C/200°C fan.

2. Heat a small frying pan over a medium heat. Add the pine nuts and toast them for 1–2 minutes until golden. Set aside.

3. Put the squash in a roasting tray with the thyme. Season with salt and pepper and drizzle with 2 tbsp extra virgin olive oil. Toss together. Roast for about 25 minutes until golden brown and caramelised.

4. While the squash is roasting, pour the stock into a saucepan and bring to a very gentle simmer.

5. Heat the remaining 2 tbsp extra virgin olive oil in a large saucepan over a medium heat. Add the onion, garlic and oregano and season with salt and pepper. Cook gently for 3–5 minutes until softened but not coloured.

6. Stir in the rice and cook for 2 minutes, making sure each grain is coated in oil. Gradually add the stock, a ladleful at a time, stirring constantly for 15–20 minutes until the rice is cooked but still has a tiny bit of bite (you may not need all of the stock).

7. When the squash is cooked, add half to a small bowl with 2 tbsp of the stock and a drizzle of extra virgin olive oil. Mash to a paste with a fork.

8. Stir the roast squash paste, butter and Parmesan into the rice. Then gently stir in the roast squash pieces and most of the basil leaves. When it's all combined, remove from the heat.

9. Scatter over the pine nuts and reserved basil leaves to serve.

Cherry Tomato, Bacon & Chilli Pasta

Serves 4 / 20 minutes

1 tbsp olive oil
4 rashers of bacon, roughly
  chopped
2 red onions, thinly sliced
1 tsp chilli flakes
2 x 400g cans cherry tomatoes
400g penne
50g Parmesan cheese, grated
1 small bunch of basil,
  leaves picked
100g rocket
Salt and pepper

This little number is an effortless midweek meal that you can throw together with basic ingredients you probably already have lying around the kitchen. Easy to make, but so good to eat!

1. Heat the oil in a large frying pan over a medium heat.

2. Add the bacon, onion and chilli flakes and fry for 5–8 minutes until the onion has softened.

3. Add the tomatoes and season with salt and pepper. Bring to the boil, then cook over a medium heat for 10 minutes until you have a thick sauce, stirring now and again.

4. Meanwhile, cook the pasta in a large pan of boiling salted water for 1 minute less than packet instructions. Drain, saving half a mug of pasta cooking water for later.

5. When the sauce has simmered for 10 minutes, add the pasta to the sauce with a splash of its cooking water and half the cheese. Toss together and cook for 1 minute, adding more water to loosen the sauce if needed.

6. Turn off the heat and stir in the basil leaves.

7. Divide among the bowls. Serve with the remaining Parmesan and a handful of rocket leaves on top of each bowl.

Baked Meatballs with Oozy Melting Mozzarella

Serves 4–6 / 45 minutes–1 hour

5 tbsp fresh breadcrumbs
4 tbsp milk
800g beef mince
1 small bunch of flat-leaf
  parsley, finely chopped
25g Parmesan cheese, grated
1 egg
2 tbsp extra virgin olive oil, plus
  extra for oiling
Pinch of salt and pepper
2 mozzarella balls, torn into
  pieces

For the sauce
2 tbsp extra virgin olive oil
1 red onion, finely chopped
3 garlic cloves, sliced
1 tbsp dried oregano
3 x 400g cans chopped
  tomatoes
2 tsp sugar
1 small bunch of basil,
  leaves picked

To serve
400g spaghetti or crusty bread
Salad or seasonal greens

Juicy meatballs in a rich tomato sauce with oozy cheese – this one's a real crowd-pleaser. It's great served with spaghetti or a good loaf of bread to mop up the sauce. I like a big fresh salad or seasonal greens on the side. Between you and me, it also makes the most amazing meatball sub sandwich.

1. Preheat the oven to 200°C/180°C fan.

2. Put the breadcrumbs into a small bowl, pour over the milk and leave for a couple of minutes to allow the bread to soak up the liquid.

3. Mix the beef mince, parsley, Parmesan, egg, oil and salt and pepper together with the soaked breadcrumbs in a separate bowl using your hands. When you have a well-combined mixture, use wet hands to roll it into 12 large balls.

4. Lay the balls on a lightly oiled baking tray and bake for 15 minutes.

5. Meanwhile, heat 2 tbsp extra virgin olive oil in a large ovenproof pan over a medium heat. (If you don't have an ovenproof pan, you can transfer everything to an ovenproof dish after step 6.) Fry the onion, garlic and oregano with salt and pepper for 5 minutes until softened.

6. Add the tomatoes and sugar with three quarters of the basil leaves, stir together and simmer for 15–20 minutes until the sauce begins to thicken.

7. Add the baked meatballs to the sauce and simmer for a further 5 minutes. If your pan isn't ovenproof, transfer everything to an ovenproof dish.

8. Top the meatballs with the torn mozzarella. Transfer to the oven and bake for 10 minutes or until the cheese is golden and bubbly. Scatter over the remaining basil leaves and serve with spaghetti or bread and a salad or greens.

Sticky Honey & Mustard Pork Chops with Crispy Roast Potatoes

Serves 4 / 40 minutes

4 pork chops, approx. 2.5cm thick
1.5kg new potatoes, halved *(use Jersey Royals when in season)*
2 tbsp olive oil
500g asparagus
3 tbsp honey
3 tbsp wholegrain mustard
300ml cider or apple juice
2 tbsp cornflour mixed with 2 tbsp water *(optional)*
Salt and pepper

I've been lucky enough to visit and cook for some of the farmers that grow these delicious Jersey Royal potatoes and I want to get us all eating and enjoying seasonal British food. The cooking time will vary depending on the thickness of the pork, so be confident when you're cooking and play it by ear. Just cut into the chop to check it – if it's still really pink in the middle, give it a little more time.

1. Remove the pork from the fridge 20 minutes before cooking. Trim the rind and some of the fat off around the edge. Kitchen scissors work well for this. Season the pork with salt and pepper.

2. Preheat the oven to 220°C/200°C fan.

3. Put the potatoes on a large baking tray. Season with salt and pepper and drizzle with 1 tbsp olive oil. Toss together. Roast for about 35 minutes until crispy, golden and tender. Give them a stir after 20 minutes, adding the asparagus (with the woody ends snapped off) to the tray for the remaining 15 minutes of cooking.

4. Mix the honey and mustard together in a small bowl.

5. Heat 1 tbsp olive oil in large non-stick frying pan over a medium heat.

6. Fry the pork for 3–5 minutes on each side until golden, then use tongs to stand the pork up on the fatty edge for 1–1½ minutes to help crisp it up.

7. Turn up the heat, then pour in the cider or apple juice, scraping off any bits stuck to the pan. Bring to the boil, then stir in the honey and mustard mixture.

8. Reduce the heat to medium and simmer for 5 minutes until the pork is cooked and the liquid reduced by half. Stir in the cornflour mixture to thicken the sauce if needed.

9. Divide the potatoes, asparagus and pork among the serving plates. Drizzle over the sauce.

Pictured on p. 68–9

Roast Vegetable, Pesto & Mozzarella Puff Pastry Tart

Serves 4 / 35–40 minutes

1 courgette, cut into 2cm chunks
1 red and 1 yellow pepper, cut
    into 2cm chunks
2 red onions, cut into 1cm slices
1 tsp mixed herbs
1 tbsp olive oil
320g pack of ready-roll
    puff pastry
1 egg, lightly beaten
190g jar basil pesto
1 mozzarella ball
1 small bunch of basil,
    leaves picked
Salt and pepper

Salad, to serve

This dish is perfect for sharing in the summer and works just as well made with ready-roll pastry and shop-bought pesto as it does with homemade. It's also great cold the next day for lunch or even as something to make ahead for a picnic. Just wrap it in clingfilm or keep in an airtight container in the fridge for 1–2 days.

1. Preheat the oven to 220°C/200°C fan.

2. Place the veg on a baking tray with the mixed herbs. Drizzle with the oil, season and toss together.

3. Line a separate baking tray with baking paper. Unroll the pastry and lay over the tray.

4. Score a 2cm border around the edges of the pastry with a knife, making sure you don't cut all the way through it. Prick inside the border with a fork. Brush all over with the beaten egg.

5. Place the veg on the top shelf of the oven and the pastry on the middle shelf. Cook both for about 20 minutes or until the pastry is golden and crisp, then remove both trays from the oven.

6. Give the veg a stir and return it to the oven for a further 10 minutes or until it's soft.

7. Meanwhile, use the back of a spoon to press the pastry down inside the border to make space for the filling. Spread the pesto evenly across the pastry inside the border.

8. Remove the veg from oven and layer it evenly across the pesto.

9. Tear the mozzarella into small pieces and scatter over the veg.

10. Bake for a further 5–10 minutes until the cheese is melted. Scatter over the basil leaves and serve with a salad.

Pictured on p. 72–3

Spaghetti Aglio e Olio

Serves 4 / 10–15 minutes

500g spaghetti
8 tbsp extra virgin olive oil
8 garlic cloves, finely sliced
Pinch of chilli flakes
1 large bunch of flat-leaf
  parsley, finely chopped
Juice of ½ lemon
50g Parmesan cheese, grated
  (optional)
Salt and pepper

Spaghetti aglio e olio (or spaghetti with garlic and oil if you haven't mastered your Italian accent) has got to be one of the simplest and most delicious pasta dishes out there. Recipes like this sum up why I love Italian food – a few good-quality ingredients can make a breathtaking meal. This is proper fast food, which you can have on the table in 10–15 minutes.

1. Cook the pasta in a large pan of boiling salted water for 1 minute less than the packet instructions. Drain, saving 2 ladles or half a mug of pasta cooking water for later.

2. Heat the oil in a large non-stick frying pan over a low–medium heat. Add the garlic and fry 1–2 minutes, stirring constantly. It should sizzle gently – be very careful not to let it burn.

3. Turn the heat up, then add the chilli flakes, cooked pasta, parsley and half the pasta cooking water.

4. Cook for another minute, tossing together all the time. Add more pasta water if needed to loosen the sauce.

5. Squeeze in the lemon juice and give it one final toss together. Adjust the seasoning to taste.

6. Scatter over the Parmesan and give it a good twist of pepper to serve.

Cali Turkey Cheeseburgers with Smashed Avo

Makes 4 / 20–25 minutes

1 large avocado
4 brioche burger buns
Butter, for the buns
500g turkey thigh mince
2 tbsp olive oil
4 slices of Cheddar cheese
1 large tomato, cut into 4 slices
1 baby gem lettuce, leaves separated
Tomato ketchup or chilli sauce
Salt and pepper

When I was in San Francisco, we cycled over the Golden Gate Bridge to a place called Sausalito for lunch, a beautiful little place with a winding road down the hill that leads you to the bay with a killer view of the bridge. I ordered the turkey burger and it was absolutely spot on – super simple and fresh with top-quality ingredients. I always whip up this burger when I'm missing a bit of that Cali sunshine.

1. Remove the flesh from the avocado and cut into thin slices. Season with salt and pepper and set aside.

2. Slice each bun in half and spread with butter.

3. Put the turkey mince into a bowl and season with salt and pepper. Use your hands to mix together into a compact mixture.

4. Divide the mixture into 4 even-sized pieces, then use wet hands to roll into balls. Press each ball down to flatten into a burger patty about 1cm thick. Season the outside of the burgers, then drizzle with a little olive oil.

5. Heat a non-stick frying pan over a medium heat. Place the buns in, buttered-side down, and toast for 1 minute until just golden. Set aside.

6. Return the pan to the heat and add the remaining oil. Fry the burgers for about 4 minutes on each side until golden and cooked all the way through. Then lay a slice of cheese on top of each burger and add a splash of water to the pan. Cover with a lid or foil and cook for 1 minute or until the cheese has melted.

7. Lay a slice of tomato and lettuce on the base of each bun. Top with the burger and avocado. Spread your sauce over the inside of each lid, place on top of the burgers and serve.

Panacalty

Serves 4 / 1 hour 15 minutes

50g butter
4 onions, thinly sliced
1kg Maris Piper potatoes, cut
  into 2mm slices
300g carrots, cut into
  2mm slices
350–500g corned beef,
  crumbled
400ml shop-bought beef gravy
50g Cheddar cheese, grated
Salt and pepper

Seasonal vegetables, to serve

Panacalty is a traditional dish from the northeast that I just had to squeeze in here. This old-school dinner is a proper winter warmer. The recipe will differ depending on who you ask but it's generally made with potatoes, onions, gravy and corned beef or leftover meat from a roast. Some people turn their noses up at corned beef but they're definitely missing a trick. The combination of corned beef and onion always reminds me of my grandad's corned beef and onion pie. So, this one's for you Grandad!

1. Preheat the oven to 200°C/180°C fan.

2. Melt the butter in a large frying pan (ovenproof if you have it).

3. Add the onion, season and cook for 5–10 minutes until softened. Remove from the pan on to a plate.

4. In a large ovenproof dish or using the same frying pan if it is ovenproof, lay one third of the potato and carrot evenly over the base, then top with half the onion and half the corned beef.

5. Repeat the process with another third of the potato, the remaining onion and corned beef, then pour in the gravy. If the gravy is really thick, add a splash of water.

6. Top with the remaining potato and season with salt and pepper.

7. Cover tightly with foil and bake in the oven for 50 minutes.

8. Remove from the oven and increase the oven temperature to 220°C/200°C fan. Scatter over the cheese and bake for a further 15 minutes or until golden and bubbly. Serve with seasonal veg.

Fish Gratin

Serves 4 / 25–30 minutes

600ml full fat or semi-skimmed
  milk
400g smoked haddock (fresh
  or frozen)
150–200g raw king prawns
50g butter
3 leeks, thinly sliced
50g plain flour
2 tbsp wholegrain mustard
350g frozen peas, defrosted
Zest and juice of 1 lemon
2 white bread buns, torn into
  2cm pieces
25g Cheddar cheese, grated
Salt and pepper

Seasonal vegetables, to serve

Smoked haddock and prawns in a creamy leek sauce with a crispy bread topping – sure to become a fast family favourite in your weeknight dinner rota. I've used fresh fish but frozen works just as well – it will just take another 10 minutes or so of cooking. The topping is a great way to use any bread that's going stale too – waste not, want not!

1. Pour the milk into large saucepan over a medium heat, add some pepper and bring to a simmer.

2. Add the smoked haddock and simmer for 5 minutes, then add the prawns and simmer for a further 3 minutes or until the fish is cooked and flaking apart. Remove the fish and prawns to a bowl using a slotted spoon, reserving the milk in the pan.

3. When the fish is simmering, melt the butter in a large non-stick frying pan (ovenproof if you have it) over a medium heat. Add the leeks, season and cook for 5–8 minutes until softened.

4. When the leeks are soft, scatter in the flour. Cook for 1–2 minutes, stirring constantly; it will turn into a paste-like mixture. Then gradually add the cooking milk from the fish, stirring constantly until you have a smooth sauce.

5. Add the mustard and peas and simmer for 3 minutes or until thick.

6. Now preheat the grill to high.

7. Add the haddock and prawns to the sauce with the lemon zest and half of the juice. If your pan isn't ovenproof, transfer the mixture to an ovenproof dish.

8. Scatter the bread over the top, followed by the cheese.

9. Pop under the grill for 5 minutes or until golden, then leave to cool for 5 minutes before serving with a squeeze more lemon and some seasonal veg.

Crispy Cornflake Chicken Burgers with Homemade Slaw

Serves 4 / 45 minutes

For the burgers

4 tbsp plain flour
2 eggs, lightly beaten
150g cornflakes, lightly
  crushed
4 skinless chicken breasts
4 tsp smoked paprika
4 tbsp mayonnaise
1 tbsp sriracha sauce (optional)
4 large burger buns, halved
1 baby gem lettuce, shredded
Salt and pepper

For the slaw

½ sweetheart cabbage,
  finely sliced
1 red onion, finely sliced
2 carrots, grated
2 tbsp plain yoghurt
1 tbsp mayonnaise
Juice of 1 lemon
2 tsp sugar

Using cornflakes to coat the chicken before baking it gives you all the crunch you'd expect from deep-fried chicken but without the grease! My lighter spin on this high-street favourite is a winner. If you've got some sriracha, mix it with the mayo for an epic burger sauce with a spicy kick.

1. Preheat the oven to 220°C/200°C fan.

2. Lay the flour, egg and cornflakes on 3 separate plates.

3. Lay the chicken on a board. Season all over with salt, pepper and the smoked paprika.

4. Dip each chicken breast into the flour. Dust off any excess, then dip in the egg, allowing any excess to drip off before evenly coating in the cornflakes. Give the cornflakes a good press down so that they stick to the chicken.

5. Put the cornflake-coated chicken on a baking tray. Bake for 30–35 minutes until crispy and cooked all the way though with no pink remaining in the middle.

6. When the chicken is cooking, make the slaw by mixing all the ingredients together in a large bowl with a pinch of salt and pepper.

7. If making the sriracha mayo, in a small bowl mix together the mayo and siracha .

8. Load each bun with lettuce, chicken and mayo. Serve with a side of slaw.

Steak & Chips with Easy Cheesy Mushroom Sauce

Serves 2 / 45 minutes

For the chips

2 Maris Piper potatoes, skin on,
    cut into 1cm-thick chips
Olive oil
Salt and pepper

For the steak

2 rib-eye steaks
1 tbsp olive oil
2 garlic cloves
2 sprigs of rosemary
40g butter

For the sauce

300g chestnut mushrooms,
    sliced
1 tbsp balsamic vinegar
200ml beef stock
3 tbsp cream cheese

You just can't beat a good steak and chips, especially with my easy cheesy mushroom sauce. This is the perfect date night supper!

1. Remove the steak from the fridge 20 minutes before cooking.

2. Preheat the oven to 220°C/200°C fan.

3. Put the chips on a baking tray. Drizzle with oil, season with salt and toss together. Roast for 40–45 minutes until golden and crisp, turning after 20 minutes.

4. Rub the steaks with the olive oil and season all over with salt and pepper.

5. When the chips have 15 minutes of cooking left, heat a large non-stick frying pan over a high heat.

6. Add the steaks to the pan with the garlic and rosemary. Fry for 2 minutes on each side until golden and caramelised, turning just once.

7. When the steaks are almost done, add the butter to the pan. When it has melted, tilt the pan and use a spoon to baste the steaks with the butter.

8. Remove the steaks to a plate and spoon over some of the butter. Cover with foil to rest. Discard the garlic and rosemary.

9. Return the pan to the heat. Add the mushrooms, season and fry for 3 minutes until softened.

10. Pour in the balsamic vinegar and let it bubble away for 30 seconds. Add the stock and stir in the cream cheese. Simmer for 2–3 minutes until you have a thick sauce. Pour in any resting juices from the steak. Remove from the heat.

11. Serve the steak and chips with a good drizzle of sauce.

Sausage & Mash with Homemade Onion Gravy

Serves 4 / 30 minutes

8–12 Cumberland sausages
  (2–3 per person)
100g butter

For the gravy
50g butter
4 red onions, finely sliced
1–2 tsp white or brown sugar
4 tbsp balsamic vinegar
500ml beef stock
1 tbsp cornflour mixed with
  1 tbsp water
Salt and pepper

For the mash
1–1.5kg Maris Piper potatoes,
  peeled and chopped into
  3cm pieces
1 tbsp mustard *(optional)*
50–100g butter

A comfort food classic! You can't beat a good homemade onion gravy and my recipe is dead easy to make. I'm partial to Cumberland sausages and have used them here, but you can choose your favourite and adjust the cooking time according to the packet instructions.

1. Preheat the oven to 200°C/180°C fan.

2. Lay the sausages on a baking tray and prick each one a few times with a fork. Bake for 20–25 minutes until cooked with no pink remaining in the middle.

3. Meanwhile, make the gravy and mash. To make the gravy, melt the butter in a saucepan over a low–medium heat. Add the onion and sugar and season generously. Cover loosely and cook for 10–15 minutes until softened and caramelised, stirring now and again.

4. When the onion is soft, turn the heat up to high and add the balsamic vinegar. Let most of the liquid bubble away – it will take about 30 seconds – then pour in the stock. Bring to the boil, then reduce the heat and simmer for 10 minutes. Adjust the seasoning to taste, then stir in the cornflour mixture a little at a time until thickened. You may not need it all.

5. For the mash, cook the potatoes in a large pan of boiling salted water for about 15 minutes until tender and cooked all the way though. An easy way to test if they are ready is to stick a knife into the potato and lift it up; if it slides off, it's done.

6. Drain the potatoes. Let them sit in the colander for 2 minutes to steam dry, then return them back to the pan. Season the potatoes with salt and pepper and stir in the mustard and butter, adding more for a richer flavour. Mash until smooth.

7. Serve a good dollop of mash with the sausages, then pour over the gravy.

Panzanella

Serves 4-6 / 5 minutes

300g ciabatta, torn into chunks
700g ripe tomatoes, chopped
1 cucumber, chopped
1 small red onion, finely sliced
Handful of pitted black olives
1 large bunch of basil, leaves
  picked
10 tbsp extra virgin olive oil,
  plus extra for drizzling
3 tbsp red wine vinegar
Salt and pepper

Panzanella is a Tuscan bread salad, perfect for using up any bread that might be going a bit stale. Use the best-quality, ripest tomatoes you can get for this one – the juicier the better. You can serve it straight away or leave it for a few hours for the bread to soak up all of the flavours. This is great as a main meal or a nice addition to bring along to any BBQ as a side.

1. Place all the ingredients in a large mixing bowl with a pinch of salt and pepper, saving a few basil leaves to garnish.

2. Give it a good mix together with your hands, evenly coating everything in oil and vinegar.

3. Taste, adding more seasoning, oil or vinegar if needed.

4. Eat straight away or let sit for 30 minutes to a few hours to allow the bread to soak up the flavours.

5. Serve with a drizzle more oil and the reserved basil leaves.

Chicken Cobbler

Serves 4 / 50 minutes

For the filling

1 tbsp olive oil
2 garlic cloves, chopped
2 tsp dried rosemary
2 leeks, finely sliced
4 skinless chicken breasts, cut
  into small chunks
300g chestnut mushrooms,
  halved
2 tbsp wholegrain mustard
500ml chicken stock
1 tbsp cornflour mixed with
  1 tbsp water
Salt and pepper

For the cobbler

300g self-raising flour
2 tsp dried rosemary
75g cold butter, diced
175ml semi-skimmed milk

This hearty meal is perfect for a cold autumn or winter's evening. Juicy chicken in a leek and mushroom sauce with a light and fluffy savoury scone topping. Good stuff.

1. Preheat the oven to 240°C/220°C fan.

2. Heat the oil in a large non-stick frying pan over a medium heat. Fry the garlic, rosemary and leeks for 5 minutes until softened.

3. Turn up the heat, add the chicken, season with salt and pepper and cook for 2 minutes until the edges of the chicken are sealed. Add the mushrooms and cook for a further 2 minutes.

4. Stir in the mustard and stock. Reduce the heat to low. Cover loosely and simmer for 15 minutes. Then stir in the cornflour mixture to thicken the sauce.

5. While the chicken is simmering, make the cobbler. Sift the flour into a mixing bowl. Stir in the rosemary with a pinch of salt and pepper. Add the butter, then use your fingertips to rub it into the flour until it resembles breadcrumbs

6. Gradually add the milk, mixing with your hands until you have a stiff dough. You may not need all of the milk. As soon as it comes together, form it into a ball.

7. Lightly flour a work surface. Use a rolling pin to roll out the dough until it is 5mm thick. Use a small cutter or knife to cut into 8cm discs.

8. Transfer the cooked chicken mixture to a medium-sized ovenproof dish. Lay the discs over the top, then lightly bush with milk.

9. Bake in the oven for 20 minutes or until the dough has risen and is nicely golden brown.

CHAPTER 3

Fakeaway

Satay-Style Chicken Curry

Serves 4 / 15–20 minutes

2 tbsp vegetable oil
4 skinless chicken breasts, cut
    into 2cm pieces
2 garlic cloves, finely chopped
3cm piece of fresh ginger,
    peeled and finely chopped
1 red chilli, finely chopped
2 onions, roughly chopped
1 red and 1 green pepper,
    roughly chopped
225g can water chestnuts,
    drained (optional)
Juice of 1 lime
1 small bunch of coriander,
    chopped

Jasmine rice, to serve

For the sauce

2 x 400ml cans coconut milk
4 tbsp smooth peanut butter
4 tbsp honey
2 tbsp medium curry powder
2 tsp ground turmeric
3 tbsp dark soy sauce

This is my take on a chicken curry inspired by the flavours of chicken satay, which we all know and love, with a rich, creamy coconut and peanut curry sauce. If you can get a hold of water chestnuts, they add a nice crunch.

1. Mix all the sauce ingredients together in a bowl and set aside.

2. Heat the oil in a wok or large non-stick frying pan until smoking hot.

3. Stir-fry the chicken, garlic, ginger and chilli for 2 minutes.

4. Add the onions, fry for 1 minute, then add the peppers and water chestnuts. Stir-fry for a further 3 minutes until the veg and chicken begin to take on some colour.

5. Add the sauce, bring to the boil, then reduce the heat and simmer for 8–10 minutes until the chicken is cooked and the sauce has thickened slightly.

6. Stir in half the lime juice and most of the coriander, leaving a little to scatter on top. Taste – you may want more honey for sweetness or curry powder for heat.

7. Serve with rice and a squeeze more lime juice.

Chicken Bhuna

Serves 4 / 30–35 minutes

1 tbsp vegetable oil
2 onions, finely sliced
4 garlic cloves, grated
2.5cm piece of fresh ginger,
   peeled and grated
1 green chilli, deseeded and
   finely chopped
4 skinless chicken breasts, cut
   into 2cm chunks
2 tbsp garam masala
2 tsp medium curry powder
1 tsp ground turmeric
1 tsp mild chilli powder
3 mixed colour peppers,
   roughly chopped
2 x 400g cans chopped
   tomatoes
1 tsp caster sugar
Juice of 1 lemon
1 small bunch of coriander,
   chopped
Salt

To serve
Basmati rice
Yoghurt

This curry is perfect for a weekend curry night, or a midweek family meal for even the fussiest of eaters. The rich, tangy tomato and pepper sauce makes it perfect for kids and you can always leave the chilli out if you like a milder curry.

1. Heat the oil in a large non-stick pan over a medium–high heat.

2. Add the onions, season with salt and fry for 5–8 minutes until lightly golden, adding a splash of water if the pan becomes too dry.

3. Stir in the garlic, ginger and chilli and cook for 2 minutes.

4. Add the chicken and season with salt. Cook for 1 minute, then stir in all the spices, except 1 tbsp of the garam masala, to coat the chicken. Cook for a further 2 minutes.

5. Add the peppers and tomatoes with the sugar. Increase the heat and bring to the boil, then reduce the heat and simmer gently for 15–20 minutes until the sauce has thickened.

6. Stir in the remaining garam masala, half the lemon juice and most of the coriander, saving just a little bit to garnish. Taste and adjust the seasoning as necessary.

7. Sprinkle with coriander, squeeze over more lemon juice and serve with rice and yoghurt alongside.

Thai Green Veggie Curry

Serves 4 / 15 minutes

4 tbsp good-quality Thai green curry paste
2 x 400ml cans coconut milk
300ml vegetable stock
2 tbsp white or soft brown sugar
2 courgettes, sliced
200g Tenderstem broccoli
150g baby corn
200g sugar snap peas
1 small bunch of Thai or regular basil, leaves picked
1 lime
1 red chilli, sliced

Jasmine rice, to serve

This fuss-free, 15-minute fakeaway is a knockout. Thai paste has a host of tasty ingredients but making it from scratch takes more time, so I've used a good-quality shop-bought curry paste here – it's a great kitchen hack. This is also delicious with a few king prawns added for the last few minutes of cooking. Jasmine works a treat here to serve.

1. Heat a large non-stick frying pan or wok over a high heat.

2. Add the curry paste and stir-fry for 2 minutes.

3. Add the coconut milk, stock and sugar and stir to combine with the paste. Bring to the boil and simmer for 5 minutes.

4. Add the vegetables and simmer for 4–5 minutes until they are cooked but still retain a bit of crunch.

5. Add most of the basil leaves and the juice of half the lime. Taste, adding more sugar for sweetness or lime for acidity. Remove from the heat.

6. Serve on rice with a squeeze of lime juice, a few basil leaves and some sliced chilli.

Beef & Coconut Curry

Serves 4 / 1 hour 20 minutes

2 tbsp vegetable oil
750g stewing steak, diced into
  bite-sized pieces
1 cinnamon stick
1 star anise
2 large onions, finely sliced
4 garlic cloves, finely chopped
4cm piece of fresh ginger,
  peeled and finely chopped
1 red chilli, chopped
1 tsp ground turmeric
1 tbsp dark brown, muscovado
  or palm sugar
1 tbsp tamarind paste
1 small bunch of coriander,
  chopped
Zest and juice of 1 lime
2 tsp fish sauce
400ml can coconut milk
4 tbsp desiccated coconut
Salt and pepper

Basmati rice, to serve

Melt-in-the-mouth beef in a creamy, aromatic coconut curry sauce, this is my spin on a curry that I first had in a hawker centre on a trip to Singapore. It's a real crowd-pleaser and easy to double up on the ingredients if you're cooking for more. It's also the ideal dish to make a couple of days in advance and leave in the fridge in an airtight container for up to 2 days. The flavours develop over time, and it'll only get tastier. You can also freeze portions for up to 3 months.

1. Heat 1 tbsp of the oil in a large pan over a high heat. Add the beef, season and fry for 3–5 minutes until caramelised and browned all over. Remove from the pan.

2. Add 1 tbsp more oil to the pan and reduce the heat to medium. Add the cinnamon stick and star anise. When they sizzle, add the onions, garlic, ginger and chilli. Season with salt and cook for about 10 minutes until the onions are lightly golden and soft.

3. Add the beef back to the pan and stir in the turmeric. Cook for 1 minute.

4. Add the sugar, tamarind, half the coriander, lime zest, fish sauce and coconut milk. Give everything a good stir.

5. Reduce the heat to low. Cover and simmer for 1 hour, stirring now and again, until the beef is tender. Remove the lid for the last 15 minutes of cooking for a thicker sauce.

6. Stir in the remaining coriander and half the lime juice. Check the seasoning and adjust to your taste with more lime juice, sugar or salt.

7. Serve on rice with a scattering of desiccated coconut.

Lamb Rogan Josh

Serves 4 / 50 minutes

4 lamb steaks, diced into
  2cm pieces
5 tbsp natural or Greek yoghurt
1 tbsp vegetable oil
1 cinnamon stick
1 bay leaf
5 cardamom pods, cracked
3 onions, finely sliced
6cm piece of fresh ginger,
  peeled and grated
4 garlic cloves, grated
2 tbsp garam masala
½ tsp ground turmeric
1 tsp ground cumin
1 tsp mild or hot chilli powder,
  depending on your
  preference
4 level tbsp tomato purée
400ml water
1 small bunch of coriander,
  chopped
Juice of 1 lemon
Salt and pepper

Basmati rice, to serve

You've probably gathered by now that I love a curry and my rogan josh is another belter to add to your repertoire. For the ultimate curry night, get a few beers in the fridge and stock up on poppadums and pickles.

1. Mix the lamb with 1 tbsp of the yoghurt. Season with salt and pepper and set aside.

2. Heat the oil in a large pan over a medium heat. Add the cinnamon stick, bay leaf and cardamom pods and let them sizzle for 30 seconds.

3. Add the onions and season with salt and pepper. Cook for 10–15 minutes, covered loosely with a lid, until dark and golden, stirring now and again. Add a splash of water if the pan becomes too dry.

4. Add the ginger and garlic along with the lamb and cook for 3 minutes until the lamb is sealed.

5. Stir in all the spices, except 1 tbsp of the garam masala, and the tomato purée. Cook for 2 minutes.

6. Add the water. Cover loosely and simmer for about 30 minutes until you have a thick, almost dry, sauce. Stir in the remaining garam masala and adjust the seasoning to taste.

7. Reduce the heat to low. Stir in the remaining yoghurt and the coriander.

8. Serve with rice and a squeeze of lemon juice.

Chicken Tikka Masala

Serves 4 / 35 minutes

2 tbsp butter
3 onions, very finely chopped
 or whizzed in a food
 processor
4 garlic cloves, grated
3cm piece of fresh ginger,
 peeled and grated
2 tsp smoked paprika
2 tsp ground cumin
2 tsp ground coriander
2 tbsp garam masala
1 tbsp tomato purée
4 skinless chicken breasts, cut
 into 2cm cubes
400g can chopped tomatoes
100ml chicken stock
4 heaped tbsp ground almonds
4 tbsp Greek yoghurt, plus
 extra to serve
3–4 tbsp honey
Juice of ½ lemon
1 small bunch of coriander,
 chopped
Salt and pepper

Basmati rice, to serve

Chicken tikka masala is one of Britain's favourite dishes and I'm a fan! My easy version will give you all the flavour that you crave from your local takeaway but with the joy of cooking it from scratch.

1. Melt the butter in a large non-stick saucepan over a medium heat until foaming.

2. Add the onions with a good pinch of salt and cook over a medium heat, loosely covered, for 10–12 minutes until really soft and golden. Stir now and again. If the pan becomes dry, add a splash of water.

3. Stir in the garlic and ginger and cook for 1 minute.

4. Add all of the spices, except 1 tbsp of the garam masala, the tomato purée and 2 tbsp water. Cook for 1 minute, stirring constantly so the spices don't stick to the pan.

5. Season the chicken with salt and add to the pan, stirring to coat in the spices.

6. Add in the chopped tomatoes and stock and simmer for about 15 minutes until the chicken is cooked and the sauce has thickened.

7. Stir in the ground almonds and remaining garam masala and simmer for 2 minutes.

8. Reduce the heat right down to very low. Stir in the yoghurt and honey along with the lemon juice and half the coriander. Have a taste, adding more honey for sweetness or lemon for sourness depending on what you fancy.

9. Serve with basmati rice and a scattering of coriander.

Drunken Noodles

Serves 2 / 10–15 minutes

2 nests of flat rice noodles
  (approx. 125g)
1 tbsp vegetable oil
1 onion, thinly sliced
2cm piece of fresh ginger,
  peeled and grated
2 garlic cloves, crushed
  or grated
1 red chilli, finely chopped
Approx. 200g raw prawns
1 egg
1 handful of cherry tomatoes,
  halved
1 pak choi, cut into 1cm slices
1 small bunch of Thai or regular
  basil, leaves picked
Juice of 1 lime

For the sauce
1 tsp toasted sesame oil
1 tbsp oyster sauce
1 tbsp dark soy sauce
1 tsp fish sauce
2 tsp sugar

Also known as Pad Kee Mao, drunken noodles are a stir-fried street-food dish from Thailand. I've used regular basil and chillies, as they're easier to find than holy basil and Thai chillies, but if you're able to get these, go for it! These noodles may be drunk, but they're also ridiculously tasty and easy to make. There are many different theories for the name 'drunken' as there's no alcohol in the recipe. One of them is that they are good with a beer, but I reckon they are perfect as they are. These spicy prawn noodles are one of my all-time favourite stir-fries.

1. Prepare the noodles according to the packet instructions.

2. Mix all the sauce ingredients together in a bowl.

3. Heat a splash of veg oil in a wok or large non-stick frying pan over a very high heat.

4. Stir-fry the onion, ginger, garlic and chilli for 1 minute. Add the prawns and stir-fry for another minute until they begin to turn pink.

5. Add the egg and scramble with your spoon, moving it around the pan.

6. Add the cherry tomatoes and pak choi. Stir–fry for a further 1–2 minutes.

7. Add the noodles. Toss together and stir-fry for 2 minutes to slightly char the noodles and get them piping hot.

8. Pour in the sauce, then throw in the basil leaves. Give everything a good toss together to evenly coat the noodles in the sauce. Remove from the heat and serve with a squeeze of lime juice.

Crispy Chilli Beef

Serves 2 / 15–20 minutes

2 x 200g rump steaks, cut into
   thin strips
50g cornflour
4 tbsp veg oil
6 spring onions, finely chopped

Long-grain rice, to serve

For the sauce
1 tbsp veg oil
4 garlic cloves, finely chopped
3cm piece of fresh ginger,
   peeled and finely chopped
1 red chilli, finely chopped
4 tbsp hoisin sauce
4 tbsp white wine vinegar
Zest and juice of 2 large
   oranges
3 tbsp sweet chilli sauce
2 tbsp dark soy sauce

This is my take on a popular dish in Cantonese restaurants and I just love how the sweet, spicy, sticky sauce clings to the crispy fried beef! I've ditched the deep-fryer to make it even easier, so why not give the takeaway a miss this weekend and whip it up at home. Don't forget the prawn crackers!

1. Pat the beef dry with kitchen paper, then toss in the cornflour and set aside.

2. To make the sauce, heat the veg oil in a large non-stick frying pan over a high heat. Fry the garlic, ginger and half the chilli for 1 minute, being careful not to let the garlic burn.

3. Add the remaining sauce ingredients. Bring to the boil, then simmer for 5 minutes until you have a thick, shiny sauce. Remove to a bowl,

4. Give the pan a quick clean, then get it back over a very high heat with the 4 tbsp of oil until smoking hot.

5. Add the steak. Stir-fry for 2–3 minutes until golden and crisp. You may need to do this in 2 batches depending on the size of the pan.

6. Pour in the sauce and stir to evenly coat the beef. Add half the spring onions. Cook for 1–2 minutes until it's nice and sticky. Remove from the heat.

7. Serve with rice, scattered with the remaining spring onions and chilli.

Roast Cauliflower Kebabs with Tahini Yoghurt Sauce

Makes 4 pittas / 40 minutes

1 cauliflower, cut into florets,
  leaves cut into 2cm pieces
2 tsp ground turmeric
2 tbsp extra virgin olive oil
150ml water
4 large pitta breads
4 tbsp pomegranate molasses
2 tomatoes, diced
1 jar pickled jalapeños
  (optional)
Salt and pepper

For the sauce
4 tbsp Greek yoghurt
2 tbsp tahini, plus extra
  to serve
2 tsp honey
Zest and juice of 1 lemon

This tasty meat-free meal will satisfy even the biggest carnivores in your life. It's packed with flavour and the cauliflower is nice and filling. If you haven't tried roast cauliflower before, I reckon you'll love it! As for the pomegranate molasses, that's a sweet, sour, sticky syrup and it's a game changer in these kebabs!

1. Preheat the oven to 220°C/200°C fan.

2. Put the cauliflower florets and the chopped leaves on a non-stick baking tray. Scatter over the turmeric, season with salt and drizzle with 1 tbsp extra virgin olive oil. Give it a mix, then pour the water into the tray and give it a final drizzle with the remaining 1 tbsp of oil.

3. Roast for 30–40 minutes until tender and slightly charred.

4. To make the sauce, mix together the yoghurt, tahini, honey and lemon zest with a pinch of salt. Loosen with a splash of water if needed, then stir in a squeeze of lemon juice. Adjust the seasoning and flavour to your taste.

5. Toast the pittas.

6. When the cauliflower is cooked, season then drizzle with the pomegranate molasses.

7. Load the pittas with a dollop of sauce, some tomatoes and pickles, then fill with cauliflower and serve.

Frying Pan Flatbread Pizzas

Makes 1 pizza / 35 minutes, *including resting*

100g plain flour, plus extra
  for dusting
½ tsp baking powder
2 tbsp extra virgin olive oil,
  plus extra to serve
50ml water
Salt and pepper

For the sauce
4 tbsp tomato passata
1 tbsp dried oregano
1 tbsp extra virgin olive oil

For the toppings
1 large tomato, cut into
  very thin slices
1 mozzarella ball, sliced
1 small bunch of basil,
  leaves picked

Thick or thin pizza base? It's a hotly debated topic, but I think you just can't beat a crisp, thin pizza.

1. Preheat the oven to 220°C/200°C fan.

2. In a large bowl, mix together the flour and baking powder with a pinch of salt. Add the oil and water and mix with your hands to form a smooth dough.

3. Lightly flour a work surface. Knead the dough for 2 minutes, then cover with a damp cloth or clingfilm. Set aside to rest for 15 minutes.

4. In a small bowl, mix together the sauce ingredients with a pinch of salt and pepper.

5. When the dough has rested, lightly flour a work surface. Use a rolling pin to roll the dough into a circle about the size of your frying pan, 1–2mm thick.

6. Heat a large, non-stick, ovenproof frying pan over a high heat. Add the dough to the pan and fry for 1–2 minutes on each side until golden and crisp (don't worry if it slightly goes up the sides of the pan).

7. Spread over the sauce, leaving a 2cm border for a crust, then lay on the tomatoes and cheese with half the basil leaves. Season with salt and pepper.

8. Transfer the pan to the oven and bake for 5–8 minutes until the cheese has melted. If your pan isn't ovenproof, transfer the pizza to a preheated baking tray.

9. Remove from the oven, top with the remaining basil and drizzle with extra virgin olive oil to serve.

Peri Peri Chicken with Minty Garlic Peas & Sweet Potato Wedges

Serves 4 / 50 minutes, *plus 30 minutes–2 hours marinating*

8 chicken thighs
4 large sweet potatoes, cut
  into wedges
1 tbsp extra virgin olive oil
2 tsp smoked paprika
Yoghurt or mayo

For the sauce
6 tbsp extra virgin olive oil
4 tbsp red wine vinegar
2 large garlic cloves, peeled
1 red chilli *(2 if you like it
  extra spicy)*
1 tbsp dried oregano
1 tbsp smoked paprika
1 tsp sugar
Salt and pepper

For the peas
400g frozen peas
1 tbsp extra virgin olive oil
1 garlic clove, chopped
1 red chilli, chopped *(optional)*
2 tsp mint sauce

Peri peri chicken has become a fast-food favourite and my homemade version is dead easy and packed with flavour.

1. Preheat the oven to 200°C/180°C fan.

2. Put the sauce ingredients into a food processor with some salt and pepper. Blitz into a smooth sauce. Set aside.

3. Put the chicken thighs into a large bowl with half the sauce (save the rest to serve). Mix together to evenly coat the chicken. Cover and transfer to the fridge to marinate for 2 hours. You can also leave it to marinate for 30 minutes at room temperature if you're in a rush. Remove the chicken from the fridge 30 minutes before cooking.

4. Put the potato wedges on a baking tray. Add the oil, salt, pepper and the paprika. Toss together until evenly coated.

5. Lay the marinated chicken on a baking tray, skin-side up.

6. Put the chicken and wedges in the oven. Bake for about 40–45 minutes until the chicken and wedges are both cooked. After 20 minutes, give the wedges a stir and use a spoon to baste the chicken in its own juices,

7. Meanwhile, cook the peas in a saucepan of boiling salted water for 3 minutes. Drain, leaving the peas in the colander.

8. Put the saucepan back over a medium heat and add the oil. Fry the garlic and chilli for 1 minute. Add the drained peas and mint sauce. Season, then lightly crush with a potato masher or fork.

9. Serve the chicken, sweet potato wedges and peas with the reserved peri peri sauce and a dollop of yoghurt or mayo to cool things down.

Chana Masala

Serves 4 / 35 minutes

2 tbsp vegetable oil
3 onions, finely sliced
4 garlic cloves, grated
3cm piece of fresh ginger,
  peeled and grated
1 red chill, deseeded and
  finely chopped
½ tsp ground turmeric
1 tsp ground coriander
2 tsp ground cumin
6 ripe tomatoes (*approx. 450g*),
  roughly chopped
2 x 400g cans chickpeas,
  drained
175ml boiling water
1 lemon, juice of ½ and ½ cut
  into 4 wedges
1 tsp garam masala
1 small bunch of coriander,
  chopped
Salt

To serve
Basmati rice
Chapattis

This reminds me of picking up an Indian takeaway on a Saturday night with my dad. Anyone else always look at the menu for an hour and still get the same thing? Well, this was a staple for us and the flavour always takes me right back to those family takeaway nights. It's vegan too!

1. Heat the oil in a large saucepan over a medium heat. Add the onions, garlic, ginger and chilli with 1 tsp salt. Cover loosely and cook for 10 minutes until golden brown, stirring now and again. If the mixture becomes too dry, add a splash of water.

2. Add the turmeric, ground coriander and cumin, stirring to coat the onions, then add the tomatoes. Cook for 1 minute.

3. Add the chickpeas and boiling water with a pinch of salt. Cook over a medium heat for 20 minutes, stirring now and again and crushing some of the chickpeas against the side of the pan with a wooden spoon or fork to help thicken the sauce.

4. Stir in a squeeze of lemon juice, the garam masala and chopped coriander. Season to taste.

5. Serve with rice and chapattis and a wedge of lemon.

Tasty Chicken Kebab Wraps

Makes 4 kebab wraps / 20 minutes, *plus 1–2 hours marinating*

700g chicken breast mini fillets
1 tbsp olive oil
4 large Greek-style flatbreads
  or pittas
1 small iceberg lettuce,
  shredded
4 tomatoes, diced

For the marinade
4 tbsp Greek yoghurt
4 garlic cloves, grated
2 heaped tsp ground cumin
2 heaped tsp smoked paprika
4 tsp dried oregano
Zest and juice of ½ lemon
2 tbsp extra virgin olive oil

For the tzatziki
½ cucumber
300g Greek yoghurt
 1 garlic clove, grated or crushed
1 small bunch of dill or mint,
  finely chopped
Squeeze of lemon juice
2 tbsp extra virgin olive oil
Salt

To serve
2 sliced jalapeños from a jar
  (optional)
Sweet or hot chilli sauce
Potato wedges *(optional)*

A traditional Greek gyros is cooked on a vertical spit, but most of us haven't got one of those at home! My homemade version packs in all the flavour without needing to set up a kebab shop in your kitchen. Juicy marinated chicken with homemade tzatziki, wrapped up in a soft, warm flatbread. If you're feeling peckish, serve it with some potato wedges on the side.

1. Put the chicken in a bowl with the marinade ingredients. Mix and transfer to the fridge to marinate for 1–2 hours. Remove from the fridge 20 minutes before cooking.

2. To make the tzatziki, grate the cucumber into a bowl and season with salt. Leave to sit for 2 minutes, then use your hands to squeeze out any excess liquid. Add the remaining tzatziki ingredients to the cucumber and mix together.

3. Preheat the grill to medium.

4. Heat the olive oil in a griddle or non-stick frying pan over a medium–high heat.

5. Fry the marinated chicken for around 3–4 minutes on each side until slightly charred and cooked through with no pink remaining.

6. Sprinkle the flatbreads with a little water. Warm under the grill for 1 minute on each side.

7. Spread the breads with tzatziki. Top with lettuce and tomatoes, chicken, a couple of jalapeños and a good drizzle of chilli sauce.

8. Serve with the remaining salad and tzatziki.

Pictured on p. 112–3

5-Spice Hoisin Duck & Rice Bowls

Serves 2 / 25 minutes

2 tbsp dark soy sauce
2 tbsp honey
2 duck breasts
2 tsp Chinese 5 spice
250g jasmine rice
½ cucumber, diced
4 spring onions, finely chopped
2 tsp toasted sesame oil
2 tbsp hoisin sauce
Salt

This is a mashup of duck with hoisin sauce and roast Peking duck and rice. Roasting a whole duck is a real art form and takes over a day to prep, so I've used duck breasts to keep this quick and simple. They stay super juicy and I think are best served pink.

1. Preheat the oven to 200°C/180°C fan.

2. In a small bowl, mix together the soy sauce and honey to make a glaze. Set aside.

3. Use a sharp knife to score the skin of the duck in a chequerboard pattern. Be careful not to score into the flesh.

4. Pat the duck dry with kitchen paper. Season with salt and evenly coat in the Chinese 5 spice.

5. Cook the rice according to the packet instructions.

6. Put the duck into a cold pan, skin-side down. Turn the heat to medium and cook for 3–5 minutes until the skin is golden and crispy. Turn the duck over. Pour over the glaze to evenly coat the duck.

7. If your pan is ovenproof, transfer it straight into the oven. If it's not, put the duck on a preheated baking tray. Cook for 8–10 minutes for blushing pink meat or slightly longer for well done.

8. Remove from the oven. Leave to rest for 5 minutes, then cut into thin slices.

9. Serve on top of the rice with the cucumber and spring onions. Drizzle with the sesame oil and hoisin sauce. Give it all a good mix together before getting stuck in.

Pictured on p. 116–7

Bun Cha

Serves 4 / 30 minutes

500g pork mince
1 small iceberg lettuce,
  shredded
4 carrots, grated
4 spring onions, chopped
2 red chillies, sliced
1 small bunch of Thai or regular
  basil or mint, leaves picked
300g vermicelli rice noodles
1 tbsp toasted sesame oil
1 tbsp vegetable oil

For the marinade
4 garlic cloves, chopped
1 tbsp dark soy sauce
2 tsp caster sugar
1 tbsp fish sauce
1 tsp ground black pepper
1 small red onion, finely
  chopped

For the dressing
350ml water
75g caster sugar
100ml fish sauce
Juice of 2 limes

This Vietnamese-inspired noodle recipe is super fresh with a kick of chilli. You can remove the seeds from the chilli for a less intense heat. Those little pork patties pack some serious flavour. You can cook this straight away or prep the pork in advance and let it marinate for a couple of hours in the fridge. Either way, it's delicious.

1. Put the pork mince into a bowl with all the marinade ingredients. Mix together using your hands until well combined. Roll into 12 even-sized balls. Set aside to marinate while you prep the other ingredients.

2. Put the lettuce, carrots, spring onions, chillies and basil into a bowl and toss together. Set aside.

3. Put the rice noodles into a bowl. Cover with boiling water and leave to soak for 5 minutes. Drain off the water, then add the sesame oil. Toss to stop them sticking together.

4. When the noodles are soaking, add the dressing ingredients to a small saucepan over a medium heat. Stir until the sugar has dissolved. Turn off the heat,

5. Heat the vegetable oil in a large non-stick frying pan over a medium heat.

6. Add the marinated pork balls to the pan. Use the back of a spoon to flatten them down slightly to form small patties. Fry for about 3 minutes on each side until cooked all the way though with no pink remaining. When cooked, spoon 1 tsp of dressing over each patty.

7. Divide the noodles into serving bowls, then pour over some dressing. Top with the salad and patties. Drizzle with more dressing and serve.

Baked Fish 'n' Chips with Minty Mushy Peas

Serves 4 / 45 minutes

1kg Maris Piper potatoes, skin
  on, cut into 1cm-thick chips
1 tbsp olive oil
4 tbsp plain flour
2 eggs, lightly beaten
75–100g dried breadcrumbs
1 small bunch of flat-leaf
  parsley, finely chopped
4 salmon fillets
400g frozen peas
1 tbsp crème fraîche
1 tbsp mint sauce
1 lemon, cut into wedges
Salt

My healthy home-cooked spin on a classic! I've baked the fish and the chips here to keep it nice and light. Coating the fish in a flour, egg and breadcrumbs mix works a treat to give you that seaside-ready crunchy coating with delicate flaking fish inside.

1. Preheat the oven to 220°C/200°C fan.

2. Place the chips on a baking tray. Drizzle with oil, season with salt and toss together so that they are evenly coated in oil.

3. Bake for about 40 minutes until golden, turning halfway through cooking.

4. Meanwhile, put the flour, egg and breadcrumbs on to 3 separate plates. Add a pinch of salt to the flour. Mix the parsley with the breadcrumbs.

5. Coat each salmon fillet with flour, then dip into the egg, allowing any excess to drip off. Evenly coat the fillets in the herby breadcrumbs.

6. Lay each crumbed fillet on to a baking tray and bake for 15 minutes until golden.

7. Cook the peas in a saucepan of boiling salted water for 3 minutes. Drain, then return the peas to the pan with the crème fraîche and mint sauce and season with salt.

8. Mash the peas with a potato masher or blitz in a food processor for a smoother finish.

9. Serve the fish 'n' chips with the mushy peas and a wedge of lemon.

Easy Steak Fajitas

Serves 2 / 10–15 minutes, *plus 15 minutes marinating*

2 small rump steaks, cut into thin strips, or 400g portobello mushrooms, sliced
1 tsp smoked paprika
1 tsp ground cumin
1 tsp dried oregano
½ tsp mild or hot chilli powder
1 lime
1 tbsp olive oil, plus extra for the marinade
1 red pepper, thinly sliced
1 green pepper, thinly sliced
1 red onion, thinly sliced
1 small bunch of coriander, chopped
4 large tortillas
1 small baby gem lettuce, shredded
4 tbsp soured cream
Salt and pepper

My juicy Tex Mex fajitas are a quick solution for a weeknight fix that packs a punch. Proper fast food! The recipe serves 2, but just double up on everything to feed 4. If you want to go veggie, swap the steak for sliced portobello mushrooms and cook them in the same way as the steak.

1. Put the steak or mushrooms into a bowl with the paprika, cumin, oregano, chilli and juice of half the lime, salt and pepper and a drizzle of oil. Mix together and set aside to marinate for 15 minutes. (If you're in a rush, you can skip this step.)

2. Heat 1 tbsp of oil in a large non-stick frying pan over a very high heat.

3. Add the peppers and onion, season with salt and pepper and stir-fry for 3–5 minutes until slightly charred. Remove to a plate and cover to keep warm.

4. Add a splash more oil to the pan if needed. Stir-fry the steak for 2 minutes, then add the peppers and onions back to the pan with half the chopped coriander and a squeeze of lime juice. Stir together and cook for 1 minute. Remove from the heat.

5. Warm the tortillas in the microwave.

6. Add some lettuce to each tortilla, top with the beef mixture, drizzle with soured cream and scatter with coriander to serve.

Singapore Noodles

Serves 2 / 10 minutes

100–150g vermicelli rice
  noodles
1 tbsp veg oil
1 large onion, finely sliced
1 red pepper, finely sliced
1 red chilli, finely chopped
  (optional)
200g sugar snap peas, halved
  lengthways
2 garlic cloves, grated
  or crushed
4 spring onions, cut into
  1cm pieces
2 eggs
Salt and pepper
Juice of 1 lime *(optional)*

For the sauce
1 tbsp medium curry powder
1 tbsp rice wine vinegar
1 tbsp dark soy sauce
1 tsp caster sugar
2 tsp toasted sesame oil
1 tbsp water
Pinch of white pepper

Singapore noodles remind me of late nights in Newcastle's Chinatown when I lived up north. They are so quick and easy to make at home and have become my go-to dinner after a busy day – so much flavour in so little time! You can also throw in any leftover cooked chicken or a few prawns to add some protein. I like to serve mine with a squeeze of lime juice to freshen it up.

1. Soak the rice noodles in boiling water for 3 minutes. Drain and set aside in the colander, allowing all of the water to drain off.

2. Mix all the sauce ingredients together in a small bowl.

3. Heat the veg oil in a wok or large non-stick frying pan over a very high heat.

4. Add the onion, pepper and chilli with a pinch of salt and stir-fry for 1–2 minutes until they begin to soften.

5. Add the sugar snap peas, garlic and spring onions and stir-fry for a further 2 minutes. Add a splash more oil or water if the pan becomes very dry.

6. Push the vegetables to one side of the pan. Crack the eggs into the space and stir with your spoon to scramble them for 30 seconds until they look cooked, then stir everything together.

7. Add the noodles to the pan, then pour in the sauce. Toss together and stir-fry for 2 minutes until the noodles are evenly coated in the sauce. Season to taste. Remove from the heat and serve with a squeeze of lime juice, if you like.

Yaki Udon

400g fresh udon noodles
1 tbsp vegetable oil
1 large onion, finely sliced
1 garlic clove, chopped
1 large carrot, peeled and cut into thin matchsticks
½ sweetheart cabbage, finely sliced
4 spring onions, finely chopped

For the sauce
2 tbsp dark soy sauce
1 tbsp tomato ketchup
1 tbsp honey
1 tbsp Worcestershire sauce
1 tbsp water

My spin on Japanese stir-fried noodles is ready in less than 10 minutes. The traditional dish uses condiments like mirin and tonkotsu sauce, which can be difficult to get hold of in the UK, so I've made mine with generally accessible ingredients. This dish is full of flavour with a sticky, moreish sauce that clings to the noodles. If you can't get udon, egg noodles do the job perfectly. A few shiitake or oyster mushrooms are a nice add on if you can get them – just add them with the veg.

1. Mix all the sauce ingredients together and set aside.

2. Cook the noodles in a pan of boiling water for 2 minutes. Drain and set aside.

3. Meanwhile, heat the oil in a large non-stick frying pan or wok over a high heat.

4. Stir-fry the onion, garlic and carrot for 2 minutes, then add the cabbage. Stir–fry for a further 2–3 minutes. Add a splash of water if the pan becomes very dry.

5. Add the cooked noodles to the pan with the sauce. Give it a stir to coat everything in sauce. Cook for 1 minute, then turn off the heat and scatter with the spring onions to serve.

Lamb Dhansak with Minty Yoghurt

Serves 4 / 40–45 minutes

2 tbsp vegetable oil
4 lamb steaks, cut into 2cm
 cubes and seasoned with
 salt and pepper
2 tbsp garam masala
2 large onions, finely sliced
4 garlic cloves, grated
 or crushed
1 large sweet potato, diced
2 tsp ground cumin
2 tsp ground coriander
½ tsp ground turmeric
1 tbsp tamarind paste
500ml lamb or chicken stock
60g split red lentils
2–4 tbsp honey
1 lemon
1 small bunch of mint, leaves
 finely chopped

Basmati rice, to serve

For the minty yoghurt
4 tbsp Greek yoghurt
½ bunch of mint, leaves
 finely chopped
Squeeze of lemon juice
2 tsp honey
½ tsp ground cumin
Salt

This has to be one of my favourite curries in the book – it's super aromatic, sweet and sour. The sort of thing the neighbours can small down the street when it's cooking. I've been making this for years and when I go home to visit my folks, we always have it served with all the trimmings for a proper curry night.

1. Mix the minty yoghurt ingredients together in a small bowl with a pinch of salt and set aside.

2. Heat the oil in a large non-stick pan over a high heat. Add the lamb and fry for 2 minutes or until browned all over. Scatter with 1 tbsp garam masala, cook for another 30 seconds, then remove to a plate.

3. Reduce the heat to medium, adding a splash more oil if needed. Add the onions with a pinch of salt and cook for 5 minutes until golden, then add the garlic and sweet potato and cook for 2 minutes.

4. Add the browned lamb, then stir in the cumin, coriander and turmeric. Cook for 1 minute.

5. Add the tamarind paste, stock and lentils. Bring to the boil, then reduce the heat to low. Cover loosely and simmer for about 30 minutes until the sauce has thickened, stirring now and again.

6. Stir in the honey, juice of half the lemon, the mint and remaining garam masala. Adjust the flavour to taste with salt, lemon and honey. Remove from the heat.

7. Serve with basmati rice and the mint yoghurt, with any extras on the side.

CHAPTER 4

One Pan

Chicken Traybake with Balsamic Roast Potatoes

Serves 4 / 1 hour 15 minutes–1 hour 30 minutes

1.2kg skin-on, bone-in chicken thighs *(approx. 8–12 thighs)*
1kg new potatoes, halved
800g cherry tomatoes
1 garlic bulb, unpeeled
8 sprigs of thyme
400g can cannellini beans, drained
4 tbsp balsamic vinegar, plus extra to serve
4 tbsp extra virgin olive oil
Salt and pepper

Seasonal greens, to serve

Everyone needs a good chicken traybake recipe. This hearty family dinner is something we ate for years when I was growing up. Chuck it all in the tray, then whack it in the oven. Once it's cooked, don't forget to pop the sweet roast garlic out of its skin. Any leftovers are delicious cold the next day and will last for 2 days in the fridge in an airtight container.

1. Preheat the oven to 200°C/180°C fan.

2. Place all the ingredients into a roasting tin and season generously with salt and pepper. Mix together to coat everything in the oil and vinegar.

3. Arrange the chicken skin-side up on top of the potatoes. Cover with foil and roast for 45 minutes.

4. Remove from the oven, give it a stir and use a spoon to baste the chicken in any juices. Keep the chicken on top, skin-side up. Return to the oven for a further 30–45 minutes until the chicken is cooked through and the skin is crispy.

5. Squeeze the soft roast garlic from its skin, then serve up with a drizzle more balsamic and some seasonal greens.

Easy Prawn Paella with Garlic Mayo

Serves 4 / 30 minutes

1 tbsp extra virgin olive oil
75g chorizo, diced
2 onions, diced
1 large red pepper, diced
2 garlic cloves, chopped
350g paella rice
1 tbsp smoked paprika
950ml fish or chicken stock
400g raw king prawns
350g frozen peas, defrosted
1 small bunch of flat-leaf
  parsley, chopped
1 lemon, juice of ½, ½ cut into
  4 wedges
Salt and pepper

For the garlic mayo
2 tbsp mayonnaise
1 garlic clove, crushed
  or grated
Squeeze of lemon juice

My easy prawn paella is a fuss-free one-pan wonder – so much flavour with very little effort. That's what one-pan cooking is all about. The little garlic mayo is dead simple and really sets it off!

1. Mix together the mayo, grated garlic and a squeeze of lemon juice and set aside.

2. Heat the oil in a large non-stick frying pan over a medium heat.

3. Fry the chorizo, onion, pepper and garlic with a pinch of salt and pepper for 5 minutes until the onion has softened and the oils have been released from the chorizo.

4. Stir in the rice and paprika and cook for a couple of minutes, coating each grain of rice in the oil.

5. Add the stock, increase the heat and bring to the boil. Reduce the heat to medium–low, cover loosely and simmer for about 15 minutes, stirring now and again. If it becomes very dry, add a splash of water.

6. Stir in the prawns and peas and cook for 5 minutes or until the prawns are pink. Stir in the parsley and lemon juice.

7. Serve with a wedge of lemon and dollop of garlic mayo.

Ale-Steamed Mussels

Serves 2 as a main or 4 as starter / 10 minutes

1kg mussels
1 tbsp olive oil
2 shallots, finely chopped
2 garlic cloves, chopped
2 sprigs of rosemary, chopped
1 tbsp Dijon mustard
500ml bottle of ale
1 small bunch of flat-leaf
   parsley, chopped
Salt and pepper

Small loaf of crusty bread,
   to serve

If you don't know where to start with mussels, this one's for you! It might sound like an intimidating dish to tackle, but when it comes down to it, cooking mussels couldn't be easier. They taste epic, don't cost a fortune and are a sustainable source of protein. They also look pretty impressive when you serve them up in a big bowl. My favourite part? Mopping up the sauce with crusty bread.

1. Rinse the mussels in cold water. Discard any that are open and don't close when you tap them on a work surface.

2. Heat the oil in a high-sided pan over a medium–high heat.

3. Add the shallots, garlic and rosemary to the pan and season with salt and pepper. Cook for 2–3 minutes until softened, then stir in the mustard and pour in the ale.

4. Bring to the boil, then add the mussels and cover with a lid.

5. Cook for 2–3 minutes until the mussels open, shaking the pan now and again, then stir in most of the parsley.

6. Discard any mussels that are closed.

7. Serve in bowls, scattered with the remaining parsley and with crusty bread alongside for dipping.

Spiced Veggie Pilaf with Fried Halloumi

Serves 4 / 25–30 minutes

5 tbsp extra virgin olive oil, plus
extra for drizzling
2 garlic cloves, sliced
2 red onions, diced
2 red, yellow or orange peppers,
diced
2 courgettes, diced
400g can chickpeas, drained
1 lemon, juice of ½, ½ cut into
thin slices
Handful of dried apricots,
chopped, or sultanas
1 tbsp ground cumin
½ tsp ground cinnamon
75ml water
2 x 250g packets of basmati or
long-grain microwave rice
1 small bunch of coriander or
flat-leaf parsley, chopped
250g halloumi cheese, cut into
5mm slices
Handful of flaked almonds (any
unsalted nuts will work)
2 tbsp honey
Salt and pepper

My spiced veggie pilaf is delicious and a great recipe to adapt for using up leftovers. You can swap the microwave rice for any you have left over from a curry and just use whatever veg you have in the fridge. If you don't have halloumi, a dollop of yoghurt on top works a treat.

1. Heat 4 tbsp of the oil in a large non-stick pan over a medium heat. Add the garlic and fry for 30 seconds.

2. Add the chopped vegetables. Season and cook for 5 minutes. Add the chickpeas, sliced lemon and fruit and cook for a further 5–10 minutes until the vegetables have softened and taken on a little bit of colour.

3. Stir in the spices along with the water and cook for 30 seconds.

4. Next, stir in the rice. You can add another splash of water here if the pan is very dry. Cover and cook over a medium–high heat for 5–8 minutes, stirring every minute or so until the rice is piping hot.

5. When the rice is piping hot, stir in most of the chopped herbs with the juice of half a lemon.

6. Divide the rice among the serving plates or pile on to a large platter.

7. Put the pan back over the heat, turning it high with 1 tbsp of oil. Fry the halloumi for 1 minute on each side until golden.

8. Lay the fried halloumi over the top of the rice and scatter over the flaked almonds and remaining herbs. Drizzle with honey and a touch more oil.

Honey & Harissa Spatchcock Chicken

Serves 4 / 1 hour–1 hour 15 minutes

1kg Maris Piper potatoes, cut
  into chunky wedges
1 large chicken, roughly 1.7kg
3 tbsp harissa paste
3 tbsp honey
Zest of 1 lemon, plus juice of ½
1 small bunch of coriander,
  chopped
6 spring onions, sliced
Salt and pepper

Salad or greens, to serve

For the dip
4 tbsp Greek yoghurt
Squeeze of lemon juice
Squeeze of honey

A sticky, sweet and spicy spin on chicken and chips –
unexpected but delicious. Spatchcocking a chicken is a great
way to speed up the cooking time and get a nice crispy skin.
It's great for a big Sunday roast, served with a big salad or your
favourite greens.

1. Preheat the oven to 200°C/180°C fan.

2. Put the potato wedges into a large roasting tray.

3. To spatchcock the chicken, lay it down on a board, breast
    down. Use sharp scissors to cut all the way up each side of the
    backbone, then discard the bone.

4. Flip the chicken back over so it's breast-side up, then press
    down using the heel of your hand until you hear a crack. Then
    open out the legs of the bird so it's flat on the board.

5. Place the chicken on top of the wedges in the roasting tray.

6. In a small bowl, mix together the harissa, honey, lemon zest
    and juice and season with salt and pepper. Pour the mixture
    over the chicken and wedges and mix with your hands so
    everything is evenly coated.

7. Cook in the oven for about 1 hour depending on the size of the
    bird or until the chicken is crispy and cooked through with no
    pink remaining. After 40 minutes, remove from the oven, turn
    the wedges over and use a spoon to baste the chicken in the
    cooking juices.

8. Mix together the ingredients for the dip.

9. When the chicken is cooked, scatter over the coriander and
    spring onions and serve with the dip and a big salad or greens.

Pictured on p. 138–9

One-Pan Lemon Sole

2 tbsp olive oil
2 garlic cloves, sliced
2 red onions, cut into
   1cm slices
3 mixed colour peppers,
   thinly sliced
4 tomatoes, quartered
10 pitted black olives
Zest and juice of 1 lemon
1 small bunch of basil,
   leaves picked
250ml white wine
4 fillets of lemon sole
Salt and pepper

To serve
Drizzle of extra virgin olive oil
Crusty bread

This summer dinner is perfect for al fresco dining. It's my spin on a classic Italian recipe called *Pesce all'acqua pazza*, which translates as 'fish in crazy water'. Traditionally the fish would be cooked in seawater, but I've gone for a drop of white wine! I love to use lemon sole as it's not something we cook often at home and its delicate flavour goes well with summery ingredients, but any fillets of white fish will work just as well.

1. Preheat the oven to 220°C/200°C fan.

2. Heat the oil in a large non-stick, ovenproof frying pan over a medium–high heat.

3. Fry the garlic for 1 minute, then add the onions, peppers, tomatoes and olives. Season with salt and pepper. Cook for 10–12 minutes until the veg begins to soften.

4. Add the lemon zest with half the basil along with the wine.

5. Bring to the boil, then reduce the heat and simmer for 5 minutes.

6. Place the fish on top of the veg and season with salt and pepper. Transfer to the oven for 12–15 minutes until the fish is cooked.

7. Scatter over the remaining basil leaves and give it a good squeeze of lemon juice and a drizzle of extra virgin olive oil. Serve with crusty bread to mop up the juices.

Pictured on p. 142–3

Lamb Orzo

Serves 4 / 35 minutes

1 tbsp olive oil
1 bay leaf
1 cinnamon stick
4 lamb steaks, cut into bite-
   sized pieces
2 small onions, diced
4 garlic cloves, sliced
8 pitted black olives, halved
1 heaped tbsp smoked paprika
1 tbsp dried oregano
150ml red wine
600ml lamb stock
400g can chopped tomatoes
400g orzo
1 small bunch of mint, leaves
   finely chopped
50g Parmesan cheese
Salt and pepper

Salad, to serve

This Mediterranean lamb is absolutely lush. It's proper comfort food in the winter, but also perfect on a summer's day served with a salad. If you haven't tried orzo before, it's a type of rice-looking pasta that perfectly soaks up this rich red wine and tomato sauce.

1. Heat the oil in a large saucepan or casserole dish over a medium heat. Add the bay and cinnamon and let them sizzle for 30 seconds.

2. Add the lamb, onions and garlic with some salt and pepper and fry for 3–5 minutes until the lamb and onion are brown.

3. Add the olives, paprika, oregano and wine. Stir well and cook for 2 minutes until most of the wine has evaporated.

4. Pour in the stock and tomatoes, bring to the boil, then reduce the heat and simmer for 5 minutes.

5. Stir in the orzo, cover and simmer for 15–20 minutes, stirring now and again until the orzo is tender and has absorbed most of the liquid. If it begins to look a little dry during cooking, add a splash more water.

6. Remove from the heat, stir in the mint and grate in most of the Parmesan.

7. Serve with some more Parmesan sprinkled on top and a side salad.

Arrabbiata Sausage Traybake

Serves 4 / 1 hour 10 minutes–1 hour 25 minutes

2kg cherry tomatoes
12 Italian sausages
2 tsp fennel seeds
2 tsp dried oregano
1–2 tsp chilli flakes
4 garlic cloves, sliced
2 tbsp extra virgin olive oil
Salt and pepper

Crusty bread, mashed potatoes
    or pasta, to serve

This is probably the easiest recipe in the book and one of the best! All the flavour of a spicy arrabbiata sauce in a banging traybake. The tomatoes cook down in all of the juices and with the fat from the sausages, they make the most incredible moreish sauce. Serve on mash or with some crusty bread. Any leftovers keep in the fridge for a day in an airtight container and make the best sausage sarnie ever!

1. Preheat the oven to 200°C/180°C fan.

2. Place all the ingredients into a large roasting tin or ovenproof dish. Season with salt and pepper. Mix together, coating everything in oil, then arrange the sausages on top.

3. Bake for 40 minutes, then give it a stir and turn over the sausages.

4. Return to the oven and cook for a further 30–45 minutes until the tomatoes are soft and jammy. Serve with your choice of crusty bread or mashed potatoes or stir through pasta.

Red Wine Chicken

Serves 4 / 1 hour 30 minutes

500g skinless, boneless
  chicken thighs
2 tbsp plain flour
2 tbsp olive oil
300g chestnut mushrooms,
  halved
4 rashers of bacon, chopped
1 onion, roughly chopped
2 carrots, cut into 1cm slices
2 garlic cloves, chopped
1 tbsp dried thyme
400ml red wine
250ml chicken stock
1 tbsp caster sugar
2 tsp cornflour mixed with 2 tsp
  water *(optional)*
Salt and pepper

Mashed potatoes, to serve

Winner, winner, chicken dinner! Juicy chicken thighs in a rich red wine sauce – now we're talking! Serve it up on some creamy mash for a moreish, wholesome family meal.

1. Preheat the oven to 200°C/180°C fan.

2. Season the chicken, then toss in the flour. Set aside.

3. Heat 1 tbsp of oil in a large non-stick, ovenproof frying pan or casserole dish over a high heat. Fry the mushrooms for 3 minutes. Remove and set aside on a plate.

4. Heat the remaining 1 tbsp oil in the pan and reduce the heat to medium. Fry the bacon for 2 minutes, then add the onion and carrots and season with pepper. Cook for 5 minutes, then add the garlic and thyme and cook for a further 2 minutes. Remove to a plate.

5. Put the pan back over the heat with a little more oil if needed. Fry the chicken for 2 minutes on each side until golden.

6. Pour in the wine. Scrape off any bits from the bottom of the pan with a wooden spoon, then add the onion and carrot mixture. Stir in the stock and sugar and simmer for 5 minutes.

7. Cover with a lid or foil. (If you don't have an ovenproof frying pan or casserole dish, then just transfer everything to an ovenproof dish.) Bake in the oven for 45 minutes, then stir in the mushrooms and cook for a further 20 minutes, uncovered.

8. If the sauce needs thickening, pop it back on the hob over a low heat and stir in the cornflour mixture. Plate up and serve with mash.

Lamb Tagine

Serves 4 / 1 hour 45 minutes

2 tbsp extra virgin olive oil, plus
   extra to serve
600g lamb steaks, cut into
   bite-sized chunks
2 onions, diced
3 garlic cloves, sliced
3 tsp ground cumin
1 tsp mild or medium
   chilli powder
1 tsp ground cinnamon
5 carrots, cut into 2cm chunks
400g can chickpeas, drained
400g can chopped tomatoes
1 tbsp honey
450ml chicken or lamb stock
10 dried apricots, chopped,
   or 75g sultanas
½ lemon, sliced
1 small bunch of flat-leaf
   parsley, chopped
Salt and pepper

Couscous, to serve

This aromatic lamb tagine is beautiful served on some steaming hot couscous. A tagine is actually the name of the pot this Moroccan dish is traditionally cooked in, but you can make it with your regular pots and pans at home. It's the sort of thing you can chuck in the oven and just let the magic happen.

1. Preheat the oven to 180°C/160°C fan.

2. Heat 1 tbsp extra virgin oil in an ovenproof casserole dish or large non-stick frying pan over a high heat. Add the lamb, season and fry for 3–5 minutes until browned all over. Remove to a plate.

3. Reduce the heat to medium and add the remaining 1 tbsp oil to the pan. Add the onions and garlic and season with salt. Fry for 3 minutes until lightly golden.

4. Add the browned lamb and spices. Stir to coat everything in the spices and cook for 30 seconds.

5. Add the carrots, chickpeas, tomatoes, honey, stock, dried fruit and lemon slices. Season, increase the heat and bring to the boil.

6. If using a frying pan, transfer everything to an ovenproof dish. If using a casserole dish, leave it in the dish.

7. Cover with a lid or foil and bake in the oven for 1 hour.

8. Remove from the oven. Give it a stir, then return to the oven, uncovered, for a further 20–30 minutes until the sauce has thickened slightly.

9. Stir in the parsley and drizzle with extra virgin olive oil. Serve with couscous.

One-Pan Spicy Sausage Rice

Serves 4 / 35–40 minutes

300g long-grain rice
6 chorizo-style sausages
1 large onion, finely diced
1 red pepper, finely diced
1 green pepper, finely diced
2 celery sticks, finely diced
2 tsp Cajun spice mix
650ml chicken stock
6 spring onions, chopped

One-pan family dinners are the best way to get all of the flavour with none of the fuss. The best thing about cooking with sausages like this is that they're already full of spices and seasoning, so you get lots of bang for your buck. If you can't get hold of the chorizo sausages, just use whatever variety you fancy.

1. Rinse the rice in a sieve under cold running water until the water runs clear.

2. Make a slit up the side of each sausage and remove the meat from the skin.

3. Heat a large non-stick frying pan over a medium–high heat. Add the sausage meat and break it up with a wooden spoon into small pieces. Fry for 3–5 minutes until golden.

4. Add the chopped vegetables and cook for a further 5 minutes until softened. Next, stir in the Cajun spice mix.

5. Add the rice. Stir to coat each grain in the fat from the sausages.

6. Pour in the stock and bring to the boil. Cover with a lid, reduce the heat and simmer for 15–20 minutes, stirring now and again, until the rice has absorbed the stock.

7. Scatter over the spring onions and serve.

Saucy Sausage &
Bean Casserole

Serves 4 / 45 minutes

2 tbsp olive oil
8 pork sausages
2 garlic cloves, sliced
1 tbsp dried rosemary *(other
  dried herbs will work)*
1 red pepper, cut into
  1cm slices
2 red onions, cut into
  1cm slices
1 tbsp tomato purée
300ml chicken or
  vegetable stock
400g can chopped tomatoes
400g can cannellini beans
Salt and pepper

Bread or mashed potatoes
  to serve

Sausage and beans is classic comfort food, and this winter warmer is an absolute (excuse the pun) banger. It's great value for money too, and you can plate it up with some bread or mash for a more substantial meal.

1. Heat 1 tbsp olive oil in a large pan over a medium–high heat.

2. Fry the sausages for 2-3 minutes until golden all over, then remove to a plate.

3. Add 1 tbsp of oil to the pan, then add the garlic and rosemary and fry for 30 seconds. Next, add the pepper and onions and season with salt and pepper. Cook for 5–10 minutes until softened.

4. Stir in the tomato purée and cook for 30 seconds.

5. Add the stock, tomatoes and beans with the liquid from the tin. Bring to the boil, then add the sausages. Cover loosely, reduce the heat and simmer for 30 minutes until you have a thick, rich sauce.

6. Serve with some bread or mashed potatoes.

One-Pan Spring Chicken & Greens

Serves 4–6 / 1 hour

2 tbsp olive oil
1kg skinless, boneless
  chicken thighs
4 leeks, thinly sliced
2 garlic cloves, sliced
650ml chicken stock
320g frozen peas, defrosted
2 baby gem lettuces, cut
  into wedges
2 tbsp crème fraîche
Salt and pepper

Crusty baguette or potatoes,
to serve

This creamy one-pan wonder is a joy to eat in the spring. It's another one of my family recipes created with M&S Food, and is perfect served with a crusty baguette to mop up the sauce or a few spuds on the side.

1. Heat 1 tbsp olive oil in a non-stick, ovenproof frying pan or casserole dish over a medium–high heat,

2. Season the chicken thighs and fry for around 2 minutes on each side until golden – you may need to do this in 2 batches. Remove from the pan to a plate.

3. Drain off any excess fat from the pan, then add 1 tbsp of olive oil. Add the leeks and garlic, season and fry for 3–5 minutes until softened.

4. Return the chicken to the pan, pour in the stock and simmer gently for 30–40 minutes until the chicken is cooked through and the sauce has reduced slightly.

5. Preheat the grill to high. If you don't have an ovenproof pan, skip this step and simmer for a further 2 minutes in the pan or transfer everything to an ovenproof dish.

6. Stir in the peas, then place the lettuce wedges around the chicken. Pop the pan under the grill for 3–5 minutes to slightly char the lettuce.

7. Stir in the crème fraîche, adding extra for a creamier sauce if you want. Serve with bread or potatoes.

Creamy Paprika Chicken

Serves 4 / 45 minutes

1 tbsp olive oil
4 skinless chicken breasts
2 onions, diced
2 red peppers, diced
2 garlic cloves, chopped
3 tbsp smoked paprika
100ml chicken stock
2 x 400g cans chopped
    tomatoes
2–4 tbsp soured cream, plus
    extra to serve
Salt, pepper and sugar

2 x 250g packets wholegrain
    microwave rice, to serve

This one-pan dinner is my take on a Hungarian paprikash. I've used chicken breasts rather than the traditional thighs as they stay nice and juicy when they cook in the creamy paprika sauce. Serve with speedy shortcut microwave rice to save on the washing up, but this also works a treat with mash or pasta too.

1. Heat the oil in a large non-stick frying pan or casserole dish over a medium–high heat. Season the chicken and fry for 2–3 minutes each side until golden. Remove from the pan to a plate.

2. Add the onions, peppers and garlic to the pan. Season and fry for 5–8 minutes until softened and the onions have taken on a little bit of colour.

3. Stir in the smoked paprika and cook for 30 seconds, then pour in the stock and tomatoes and season with salt and pepper and a pinch of sugar. Bring to the boil.

4. Add the chicken back to the pan, then reduce the heat. Cover loosely and simmer for 25–30 minutes or until the chicken is cooked all the way through with no pink remaining. Turn the chicken over after 15 minutes of cooking. Give the sauce a stir now and again.

5. When the chicken is cooked, reduce the heat and stir in the soured cream.

6. Serve with the rice and a drizzle more soured cream.

CHAPTER 5

Feeding a Crowd

Easy Tomato & Smoked Paprika Chicken

Serves 4–6 / 2 hours

3 tbsp olive oil
1.2kg chicken drumsticks
1 cinnamon stick
2 bay leaf
2 onions, cut into 1cm slices
1 red, 1 orange and 1 yellow
  pepper, cut into 1cm slices
3 garlic cloves, sliced
1 tbsp tomato purée
2 tbsp smoked paprika
150ml white wine
2 x 400g cans chopped
  tomatoes
1 chicken stock cube mixed
  with 250ml boiling water
Handful of pitted black olives
1 small bunch of flat-leaf
  parsley, chopped
Salt and pepper

To serve
Basmati rice
Crusty bread

These juicy, melt-in-the-mouth chicken drumsticks, cooked slowly in a rich tomato sauce flavoured with smoked paprika and olives, are my spin on a recipe from the Basque Country and the perfect sharer. Serve this dish with rice and a crusty loaf to mop up the sauce.

1. Preheat the oven to 200°C/180°C fan.

2. Heat 2 tbsp olive oil in a large casserole dish or frying pan over a medium–high heat.

3. Season the chicken and fry for 3-5 minutes until golden brown all over – do this in 2 batches if necessary. Remove from the pan to a plate.

4. Add 1 tbsp more oil to the pan with the cinnamon stick and bay leaf. Let them sizzle for 30 seconds.

5. Add the onions, peppers and garlic, season and cook for 5 minutes until the vegetables begin to soften. Stir in the tomato purée and paprika and cook for 30 seconds.

6. Pour in the wine and let most of the liquid evaporate. Add the chopped tomatoes, stock and olives, then season with salt and pepper. Bring to the boil, then reduce the heat and simmer for 5 minutes.

7. If using a casserole dish, add the chicken back to the dish and stir to submerge it in sauce. Alternatively, transfer the chicken to a large ovenproof dish or roasting tin and pour over the sauce to evenly cover the chicken.

8. Cover with foil or a lid. Cook in the oven for 1 hour.

9. Remove from the oven and give it a stir, then cook for a further 30 minutes, uncovered, until the chicken is cooked and beginning to fall apart.

10. Scatter over the parsley and serve with rice and crusty bread.

Chargrilled Lamb Steaks with Garlicky Rosemary Beans

Serves 6 / 15 minutes

6 lamb steaks
5 tbsp extra virgin olive oil, plus extra for drizzling
4 garlic cloves, sliced
6 sprigs of rosemary, leaves chopped
3 x 400g cans cannellini beans, 2 cans drained
2 chicken stock cubes mixed with 300ml boiling water
150g kale, shredded
Zest and juice of 1 lemon
Salt and pepper

It might sound a bit fancy, but this is a doddle to make and perfect for a dinner party, or even a date night for 2 – just reduce the ingredients to 2 steaks, 1 can of beans and 100ml stock. If you haven't cooked lamb steaks before, treat it like beef – I like it blushing pink in the middle.

1. Remove the lamb from the fridge 30 minutes before cooking. Season and drizzle lightly with 2 tbsp extra virgin olive oil.

2. Heat the remaining 3 tbsp extra virgin oil in a large non-stick frying pan or saucepan over a medium heat. Add the garlic and rosemary and fry for 1 minute.

3. Turn the heat up to high. Add the drained beans and the last can of beans with its liquid, along with the stock and kale. Season and bring to the boil. Reduce the heat slightly and simmer for about 10 minutes until most of the liquid has evaporated and you have a thick sauce. Add the lemon zest and half the juice.

4. While the beans are simmering, heat a large griddle or non-stick frying pan over a high heat. Fry the lamb for 2–2½ minutes on each side until caramelised. Remove to a plate, cover and leave to rest for 5 minutes.

5. Slice the lamb into thin strips. Pour any resting juices into the beans.

6. Divide the beans among the serving plates, then lay over the sliced lamb. Drizzle with oil and give them a squeeze of lemon juice to serve.

Miso Glazed Cod

Serves 6 / 20 minutes, *plus 24 hours marinating*

6 thick cod loins *(approx. 150g each)*
600g Tenderstem broccoli
2 tbsp sesame seeds

Jasmine rice, to serve *(optional)*

For the marinade
6 tbsp white miso paste
6 tbsp honey, plus extra for drizzling
6 tbsp lemon juice
1 tbsp toasted sesame oil
1 tbsp dark soy sauce

For the dressing
2 tsp white miso paste
1 tbsp honey
3 tbsp olive oil
1 tbsp toasted sesame oil
Juice of ½ lemon
2cm piece of fresh ginger, peeled and grated

One of my favourite things to order in a Japanese restaurant is black cod and this is my easy home-cooked spin on just that! Black cod is a type of fish – it can be hard to get hold of so I've used cod loin, which works well too. Try and get the thickest ones you can.

1. Mix all the marinade ingredients together in a small bowl.

2. Put the fish into a bowl and pour over the marinade, making sure the fish is evenly coated. Cover with clingfilm and transfer to the fridge to marinate for 24 hours.

3. Preheat the oven to 200°C/180°C fan.

4. Mix all the dressing ingredients together and set aside.

5. Place the marinated cod on a large baking tray lined with foil. Roast for 8 minutes, then remove from the oven and drizzle with honey. Finish cooking under a very hot grill for about 4 minutes until charred and caramelised. If you have a separate grill, preheat this when the fish goes in the oven; if it's built in, switch to the grill setting when you remove the fish to drizzle it with honey. Alternatively, if you don't have a grill you can cook it in the oven for a total of about 12 minutes, you just won't get quite as much caramelisation.

6. While the fish is in the oven, cook the broccoli in a large pan of boiling salted water for 3–4 minutes. Drain it, making sure to get rid of all the water. Put the broccoli back in the pan. Add half the dressing and toss together.

7. Serve the fish with the broccoli, a drizzle more dressing, a nice scatter of sesame seeds and the rice alongside.

Lamb Ragù with Rigatoni

Serves 4 (double up to serve 8) / 1 hour 15 minutes

500g lamb mince
1 cinnamon stick
2 onions, diced
4 garlic cloves, crushed
1 bay leaf
2 tsp dried oregano
1 tbsp tomato purée
400ml lamb stock
400g can chopped tomatoes
1 small bunch of mint,
  leaves chopped
400g rigatoni
Salt and pepper
50g feta cheese

This rich ragù with rigatoni is off the charts. It makes a nice change using lamb rather than beef, and it brings an incredible depth of flavour to this bowl of comfort food. If you double up the ingredients to make it for 8 people, you will need to simmer it for an extra 15 minutes to get that lovely thick sauce we're after.

1. Heat a large frying pan or casserole dish over a high heat.

2. Add the lamb, season and fry for 3–5 minutes until browned and caramelised. Remove with a slotted spoon to a plate, leaving the fat in the pan.

3. Reduce the heat to medium. Add the cinnamon stick, onions and garlic and season with plenty of salt and pepper. Cook for 5 minutes until softened.

4. Add the lamb back to the pan along with the bay leaf, oregano and tomato purée. Stir and cook for 30 seconds, then stir in the stock and chopped tomatoes. Bring to the boil.

5. Reduce the heat to low. Cover loosely with a lid and simmer for 45 minutes–1 hour until you have a thick, rich sauce. Then stir in the mint.

6. When the sauce is almost ready, cook the pasta according to the packet instructions. Drain, saving a little of the pasta cooking water.

7. Add the pasta to the sauce, along with a little of the cooking water to loosen the sauce if needed.

8. Divide among serving dishes, then crumble over the feta to serve.

Pictured on p. 162–3

Bean Chilli Loaded Wedges

Serves 4–6 / 50 minutes

6 sweet potatoes, skin on, cut
   into thick wedges
3 tbsp extra virgin olive oil
2 red onions, diced
2 garlic cloves, grated
   or crushed
2 celery sticks, diced
2 carrots, diced
2 red peppers, diced
1 tbsp smoked paprika
1 tbsp ground cumin
1 tsp chilli powder *(optional)*
400g can kidney beans
400g can chickpeas
2 x 400g cans chopped
   tomatoes
2 tsp brown sugar
100g Cheddar cheese, grated
Salt and pepper

To serve *(optional)*
1 avocado, sliced
6 spring onions, chopped
2 tbsp soured cream or
   yoghurt
1 lime, cut into wedges

My loaded wedges make veg the star of the show. Bang them in the middle of the table and let everyone dive in. Pick and choose any toppings you like. The more the merrier for me! I love the the contrast of creamy avo and soured cream against the rich spicy chilli and for some extra indulgence, don't hold back on the cheese.

1. Preheat the oven to 220°C/200°C fan.

2. Put the wedges into a baking tray. Drizzle in 1 tbsp oil, season and toss together. Bake for 30–40 minutes until slightly golden and cooked through.

3. Meanwhile, heat 2 tbsp oil in a large pan over a medium–high heat. Add the onions, garlic, celery, carrots and peppers. Season and fry for 10–12 minutes until the veg has softened and taken on a little colour.

4. Add the paprika, cumin and chilli powder and stir for 30 seconds.

5. Add the beans and chickpeas with the liquid from the cans along with the chopped tomatoes and sugar. Season and bring to the boil.

6. Cover loosely and simmer for 30 minutes until you have a thick, rich sauce. If the pan becomes dry during cooking, add a splash of water. Adjust the seasoning to taste.

7. Pour the chilli over the cooked wedges, then scatter over the cheese. Return to the oven for 5 minutes or until the cheese has melted.

8. Scatter over your chosen toppings and serve.

Pictured on p. 166–7

Baked Sea Bass in Black Bean Sauce

Serves 6 / 25 minutes

500g black bean sauce
12 spring onions, chopped
10cm piece of fresh ginger, cut
  into thin matchsticks
6 sea bass fillets, skin on
600g Tenderstem broccoli
1 tbsp olive oil
4 garlic cloves, sliced
2 red chillies, chopped
1–2 tbsp toasted sesame oil
1 small bunch of coriander
Salt

Jasmine rice, to serve

Baked sea bass is one of my favourite Chinese dishes, which I used to love eating on special occasions with the family that owned the Chinese restaurant I worked in as a teenager. I've kept mine simple with sea bass fillets rather than a whole fish and have teamed it up with the black bean sauce that we all know and love and chilli and garlic broccoli, plus steaming jasmine rice alongside. This serves 6 but it's easy to reduce the amounts to serve 2 or 4.

1. Preheat the oven to 200°C/180°C fan.

2. Lay 3 sheets of foil about 40cm long on the worktop.

3. Put 1 tbsp black bean sauce in the middle of each sheet of foil. Top each spoonful of sauce with a few chopped spring onions and ginger matchsticks, then lay over a fillet of sea bass, skin–side down.

4. Spread each fillet of sea bass with 1 tbsp black bean sauce, topping each with some more spring onions and ginger, then place the remaining sea bass fillets on top, skin-side up, like making a sandwich. Drizzle over a little more black bean sauce and throw in the remaining spring onions and ginger.

5. Close the foil up tightly around the fish to make 3 parcels that look a bit like Christmas crackers.

6. Lay each parcel on a baking tray and bake for 15–18 minutes until the fish is just cooked and flaking apart.

7. Meanwhile, cook the broccoli for 2 minutes in a large pan of boiling water. Drain, removing as much water as possible.

8. Heat the olive oil in a large non-stick frying pan or wok over a medium heat. Add the garlic and chilli. When they sizzle, add the broccoli with a big pinch of salt. Stir-fry for 2–3 minutes, then pour in the sesame oil, toss together and remove from the heat. You may want to do this in 2 batches depending on the size of your pan.

9. Serve 1 fillet of sea bass per person with some broccoli and rice, spooning over the sauce, spring onions and ginger from the parcels. Scatter with coriander leaves. Drizzle with more sauce.

Romesco Chicken with Crispy Lemon Potatoes

Serves 6 / 45 minutes

6 large Maris Piper potatoes,
  skin on, cut into 2cm chunks
3 tbsp extra virgin olive oil
6 chicken breasts, skin on
Zest of 1 lemon, plus a squeeze
  of juice
Salt and pepper

Seasonal vegetables or salad,
  to serve

For the sauce
450g jarred roast red peppers
3 garlic cloves
3 tbsp fresh breadcrumbs
3 tbsp red wine vinegar
6 tbsp extra virgin olive oil
75g blanched almonds

Romesco is a tasty Spanish sauce made with roast red peppers and almonds. It's dead easy to make and goes perfectly with meat and fish. If you have any left, keep it in the fridge for up to 2 days to use in salads and sandwiches.

1. Preheat the oven to 220°C/200°C fan.

2. Put the potatoes on a large non-stick baking tray. Drizzle with 1 tbsp oil, season with salt and pepper, then toss together to evenly coat in the oil.

3. Put the chicken on a separate baking tray. Season all over with salt and pepper, then lightly drizzle with the remaining 2 tbsp oil.

4. Put the potatoes in the oven and cook for 15 minutes, then add the chicken to the oven and cook for a further 25 minutes. The potatoes should be golden and crisp, and the chicken should be cooked all the way through with no pink remaining.

5. Meanwhile, put all the sauce ingredients into a food processor or high-speed blender with a good pinch of salt and pepper. Blitz until smooth. You can add more oil to loosen the sauce if needed.

6. When the potatoes are cooked, season and then add the lemon zest along with a squeeze of its juice. Toss together.

7. Serve the potatoes and sliced chicken with a good drizzle of sauce and seasonal vegetables or salad alongside.

Pork Loin with Sweet & Sour Peperonata Sauce

Serves 6–8 / 50 minutes

2 x 500g pork loin fillets
8 tbsp extra virgin olive oil, plus
 extra for drizzling
10 slices of Parma ham
6 garlic cloves, sliced
3 red peppers, thinly sliced
3 yellow or orange peppers,
 thinly sliced
4 red onions, thinly sliced
4 tbsp red wine vinegar
1 bunch of flat-leaf parsley,
 finely chopped
200g mascarpone cheese
Salt and pepper

Boiled potatoes or crusty
 bread, to serve

There's minimal work involved in this Italian-inspired feast, making it perfect for guests with a glass of wine or a nice family dinner. I've served it with a dollop of mascarpone on the side but you can mix this into the peppers when they are cooked for a nice creamy sauce.

1. Preheat the oven to 200°C/180°C fan.

2. Lay the pork onto a baking tray. Pat it dry with kitchen paper, then drizzle with 2 tbsp extra virgin olive oil and season all over with salt and pepper. Wrap the ham around the pork, then drizzle with more oil.

3. Bake for 30–40 minutes, depending on how you like your pork cooked and the thickness of the meat. Use a spoon to baste the pork in its own juices after 20 minutes. To check if it's cooked, cut into the middle of one of the fillets. I like mine slightly pink but you can cook to however you enjoy eating it. Leave to rest for 10 minutes before cutting into 1cm slices.

4. When you've put the pork in the oven, heat 6 tbsp extra virgin olive oil in a large pan over a medium heat.

5. Add the garlic, peppers and onions and season with salt and pepper. Mix together and cook for about 30 minutes, covered loosely, until soft and sweet. Stir regularly.

6. When the peppers and onions are cooked, turn the heat up to high. Add the vinegar and let it bubble away for 1 minute. Stir in the parsley, then turn off the heat.

7. Divide the peppers and onions onto serving plates, top with a few slices of the pork and add a spoonful of mascarpone on the side. Serve with boiled potatoes or crusty bread.

Chilli Prawn Linguine

Serves 4 / 10–15 minutes

500g linguine
4 tbsp extra virgin olive oil, plus
  extra to serve
2 garlic cloves, sliced
1 red chilli, deseeded
  and sliced
360g raw king prawns
250g cherry tomatoes, halved
100ml white wine *(optional)*
1 small bunch of basil,
  leaves picked
Juice of 1 lemon
Salt and pepper

Prawn linguine is the sort of dish you get in a nice Italian restaurant. It's super easy to make and tastes pretty impressive. The sauce is ready in less time than the pasta takes to cook, so it's great for a relaxed dinner with friends or an easy midweek meal. To serve 2 people, divide the ingredients in half, or to serve 6, add half as much again.

1. Cook the linguine in a large pan of boiling salted water for 1 minute less than the packet instructions. Drain, saving half a mug of the pasta cooking water.

2. Meanwhile, heat the extra virgin olive oil in a large non-stick frying pan over a medium–high heat.

3. Add the garlic and chilli. Fry for 30 seconds, then add the prawns and stir-fry for 1 minute until they start to turn pink.

4. Add the tomatoes with a pinch of salt and pepper and the wine, if using. Cook for 2–3 minutes until the tomatoes have slightly softened. Add a splash of water from the pasta if the pan begins to look too dry.

5. Add the drained pasta to the pan along with a splash of its cooking water and most of the basil. Toss together to coat the pasta in the sauce and cook for another minute. Add the lemon juice and turn off the heat.

6. Serve with a drizzle more oil and the remaining basil leaves.

Za'atar Roast Aubergine with Cumin Rice

Serves 6 / 50 minutes

3 aubergines, cut in half
    lengthways
Juice of 1 lemon
8 tbsp extra virgin olive oil,
    plus extra for drizzling
6 tbsp za'atar, plus 2 tsp
    to serve
6 tbsp plain yoghurt
1 small bunch of mint,
    leaves chopped
200g pomegranate seeds
Salt and pepper

For the rice
600g basmati rice
2 tbsp cumin seeds
2 large onions, thinly sliced
Butter (optional)

This Middle Eastern-inspired veggie recipe looks epic served on a platter in the middle of the table. Za'atar is a blend of herbs and spices with a nice zing to it. If you want a touch of indulgence, add some butter to the rice when it's cooked to take it up a notch and give it a rich, luxurious flavour.

1. Preheat the oven to 200°C/180°C fan.

2. Use a sharp knife to make a criss-cross pattern on the inside of each aubergine half, about 1cm deep.

3. Lay the aubergines on a baking tray. Pour half the lemon juice over the cut side of the aubergines. Drizzle all over with 6 tbsp oil, season with salt and pepper and scatter over 6 tbsp za'atar. Use your hands to rub the oil and za'atar all over the aubergines, getting it into the grooves.

4. Give the aubergines a final drizzle of oil and roast for about 45 minutes until soft and slightly charred on top.

5. To make the rice, weigh the rice in a measuring jug or mug. (You will need 2 x the volume of boiling water to rice for cooking later, so 1 mug of rice = 2 mugs of water.)

6. Put the rice into a sieve, rinse under cold running water until the water runs clear, then set aside. Boil the kettle.

7. Heat the remaining 2 tbsp oil in a large saucepan over a medium–high heat and add the cumin seeds. When they sizzle, add the onions with a good pinch of salt and fry for 5 minutes until golden.

8. Add the rice to the pan with double its volume of boiling water and a pinch of salt. Cover with a lid and cook for 10–12 minutes over a low heat until all of the water has been absorbed. When the rice is cooked, you can add a couple of knobs of butter for a richer flavour. Fluff up with a fork.

9. Serve the roast aubergines on top of the rice. Squeeze over the remaining lemon juice. Drizzle with yoghurt and oil and scatter over the mint, pomegranate seeds and remaining za'atar.

Creamy Garlic Mushroom Tagliatelle

Serves 6 / 15 minutes

6 tbsp pine nuts
1 tbsp olive oil
2 tbsp butter
800g chestnut mushrooms, sliced
6 garlic cloves, finely chopped
6 sprigs of thyme
250ml vegetable or chicken stock
600g fresh tagliatelle
6 tbsp crème fraîche
75g Parmesan cheese, grated
Salt and pepper

Transforming humble garlic mushrooms into a delicious creamy bowl of pasta, this veggie recipe takes just 15 minutes to cook and always hits the spot.

1. Heat a large non-stick frying pan over a medium heat. Add the pine nuts and toast for about 1 minute, stirring constantly, until lightly golden. Remove and set aside.

2. Put the pan back over the heat and turn it up to high. Add the olive oil and butter and the mushrooms, season and fry for 5–8 minutes until softened and most of the moisture has evaporated.

3. Fill a large saucepan with boiling water from the kettle to cook the pasta later.

4. When the mushrooms are soft, add the garlic and thyme. Fry for a further 3 minutes, then add the stock and simmer for 1 minute. Turn the heat down to low and stir in the crème fraîche.

5. Cook the pasta in the boiling water for 3 minutes. Drain, saving half a mug of the pasta cooking water.

6. Add the pasta to the sauce along with half the Parmesan. Add a little of the pasta cooking water to loosen the sauce if needed. Toss together to coat the pasta in the sauce.

7. Divide among serving bowls. Scatter with the toasted pine nuts and remaining Parmesan. Serve with ground black pepper.

Slow Cooked Spiced Lamb Shoulder with Lemon & Coriander Potatoes

Serves 6 / *4 hours, plus 12–24 hours marinating*

2kg lamb shoulder, bone in
1.5kg new potatoes
400ml water
Juice of ½ lemon
1 small bunch of coriander, chopped
Salt and pepper

For the marinade
300g Greek yoghurt
6 garlic cloves, grated or crushed
5cm piece of fresh ginger, peeled and grated
4 tbsp garam masala
1 tsp chilli powder
Juice of ½ lemon

For the tomato salad
6 ripe tomatoes, finely diced
1 small red onion, very finely sliced
1 small bunch of mint, leaves finely chopped
Squeeze of lemon juice

Spice up your Sunday roast with this slow-cooked lamb. I like to get it all prepped the day before and then let the oven do the hard work while I'm enjoying my guests' company – you'll look like the ultimate relaxed chef! Save any leftover lamb to put in warm flatbreads with garlic mayo and chilli sauce the next day. It's worth making just for that!

1. Mix all the marinade ingredients together in a bowl, reserving 2 tbsp of garam masala.

2. Use a sharp knife to score the lamb all over in a chequerboard pattern, about 5mm deep.

3. Put the lamb into a large dish. Pour over the marinade. Use your hands to evenly coat the lamb, getting the marinade into the grooves of the chequerboard pattern. Cover with cling film and transfer to the fridge to marinate for 12–24 hours.

4. Preheat the oven to 180°C/160°C fan.

5. Put the potatoes into a large roasting tin. Scatter with 1 tbsp garam masala and a pinch of salt. Pour in the water. Sit the lamb on top.

6. Cover tightly with foil and cook for 3 hours. Remove from the oven, baste the lamb in the pan juices, then cook, uncovered, for a further 1 hour or until the meat is tender and falling from the bone.

7. Meanwhile, mix all the tomato salad ingredients together with some salt and pepper and set aside.

8. Remove the potatoes and put them in a large bowl. Gently crush them with a fork or potato masher, keeping them intact. You just want to crush them slightly so they can soak up the flavour. Add a few spoons of the pan juices, the lemon juice, 1 tsp salt and the coriander with a pinch of garam masala. Toss together.

9. Pull the lamb apart with 2 forks in the roasting tray, coating in the pan juices.

10. Serve the lamb with the potatoes and tomato salad, drizzled with more juices from the pan.

Pan-Fried Sea Bass
with Saucy Chorizo Beans

Serves 6 / 40 minutes

4 tbsp olive oil, plus extra
  to serve
150g chorizo, diced
2 red onions, diced
400g cherry tomatoes, halved
125ml white wine or a splash of
  wine vinegar
3 x 400g cans butter beans,
  1 can drained
1 small bunch of flat-leaf parsley,
  chopped
2 lemons, juice of 1, 1 cut into
  wedges
6 sea bass fillets, skin on
Salt and pepper
Bread, to serve

A bobby-dazzler of a dinner for friends. Another recipe that sounds and looks impressive but isn't a faff to make. If you're not super confident frying fish, you can always bake it in the oven for 12–15 minutes at 200°C/180°C fan – it's still delicious!

1. Heat 2 tbsp olive oil in a large non-stick frying pan or large saucepan. Fry the chorizo for 2 minutes until the oil starts to release. Add the onions, season and cook for 5–10 minutes until softened.

2. Add the tomatoes with a pinch of salt, turn up the heat and cook for 2 minutes.

3. Add the wine and let it bubble away for a minute, then add the beans with the water from 2 of the cans and a good pinch of salt. Bring to the boil.

4. Reduce the heat and simmer for 20–25 minutes or until you have a thick sauce, then add the parsley and juice of ½ lemon. Check the seasoning. Turn off the heat and cover to keep warm.

5. Meanwhile, pat the skin of the sea bass dry, then score the skin of each fillet 2mm deep several times, a couple of centimetres apart. Season with salt.

6. When the beans have about 5 minutes of cooking left, heat the remaining 2 tbsp oil in a large non-stick frying pan over a high heat. Add the fish, skin-side down, making sure it sizzles when added. Press down gently with your fingers or a spatula to stop it curling up.

7. Cook for 2–3 minutes until the skin is crispy and golden, then flip and cook for another minute. Squeeze over the juice of ½ lemon. Turn off the heat.

8. Divide the beans between serving dishes and top each with a fillet of fish. Serve with a wedge of lemon, a drizzle of oil and bread on the side.

CHAPTER 6

Sweet

Poached Pears with Hot Chocolate & Ginger Sauce

Serves 4 / 20 minutes

4 pears, peeled
200g caster sugar
6cm piece of fresh
  ginger, sliced
350g jar crystallised stem
  ginger in syrup
275ml double cream
150g 70% dark chocolate,
  broken into small pieces

Vanilla ice cream, to serve

Chocolate and pear is a match made in heaven and this dead-easy recipe looks super impressive when you pour the hot chocolate sauce all over the pears. I love the mix of hot sauce with cold ice cream. The perfect dinner party dessert to impress without stress.

1. Cut off the base of the pears so that they can stand upright easily.

2. Fill a medium saucepan three quarters full with boiling water. Add the sugar. Place on the hob over a high heat and bring to the boil. Stir until the sugar has dissolved.

3. Add the pears and fresh ginger to the pan. Reduce the heat to medium and simmer for 15 minutes until the pears are tender.

4. Roughly chop 4 chunks of the stem ginger and set aside.

5. To make the sauce, put the cream into a small saucepan over a very low heat with the chocolate and 4 tbsp syrup from the jar of stem ginger. Stir constantly until melted.

6. Stand the pears on serving plates and add a scoop of vanilla ice cream to each plate.

7. Pour over the hot chocolate sauce, then scatter over the chopped stem ginger. Drizzle each pear with a little more syrup from the jar.

Lemon Posset

Makes 4–6 / 15 minutes, *plus 3 hours–overnight setting*

500ml double cream
125g caster sugar
Zest and juice of 2 lemons
4 small shortbread biscuits
Handful of raspberries
  (optional)

One of the easiest puds going! This tangy treat is absolutely spot on if you've got some mates coming over. You can make it 1 or 2 days ahead of time and it will be ready in the fridge when you need it. If you want to make it look a bit fancy, chuck a few raspberries on top.

1. Put the cream and sugar into a saucepan over a high heat and bring to the boil.

2. Simmer for 3 minutes, stirring as you go, to dissolve the sugar.

3. Leave to cool for 10 minutes.

4. Stir in the lemon zest and juice. Pour into ramekins or serving glasses, then transfer to the fridge to set for at least 3 hours or ideally overnight.

5. Serve with a shortbread biscuit to either dip in or crumble on top. Scatter over a few raspberries to finish, if using.

Singing Hinnies

Makes about 16 / 30 minutes

500g plain flour, plus extra
  for dusting
1 tsp baking powder
2 tbsp caster sugar, plus
  extra to serve
250g cold butter, diced, plus
  extra to cook and serve
75g currants
4–6 tbsp milk

The singing hinny is an old recipe from my home county of Northumberland and it's popular around the northeast. It's basically a griddled or pan-fried scone, and I love to eat them warm. When they're still hot, give them a good spread of butter and dusting of sugar. You can also serve them cold with more butter and jam and even some clotted cream. They will last a couple of days but are best eaten ASAP!

1. Put the flour, baking powder and sugar into a large mixing bowl and stir together.

2. Add the butter and use your fingertips to rub it into the flour until it resembles breadcrumbs. Stir in the currants.

3. Add 4 tbsp milk and use your hands to bring the mixture together into a dough. If it's very dry, add more milk until it comes together – don't overwork the mixture. As soon as it comes together to form a ball of dough, stop.

4. Lightly flour a work surface and use a rolling pin to roll out the dough until it is 5mm thick.

5. Use a small cutter (around 7cm) to cut out as many hinnies as you can, then bring the dough back into a ball, roll it out again and repeat the process until you have used all of the dough.

6. Grease a non-stick pan or griddle with butter over a medium heat.

7. Fry the hinnies for about 5 minutes on each side until golden.

8. When cooked, spread with lots of butter and dust with sugar before serving. Alternatively, leave to cool on a wire rack and serve with butter and jam.

Easy Apple Tart

Serves 6–8 / 30 minutes

1 tbsp caster sugar

4 tsp ground cinnamon

320g ready-roll puff pastry

1 egg, lightly beaten

50g butter

500g cooking apples, skin on, cut into approx. 1.5cm cubes

500g eating apples, skin on, cut into approx. 1.5cm cubes

75g sultanas

Zest of ½ lemon and 2 tbsp juice

100g light muscovado sugar

75g pecans, roughly chopped

Custard, cream or ice cream, to serve

Hot saucy apples and cinnamon on flaky puff pastry, this is a fuss-free way to serve up something sweet. The hardest bit is trying to decide if you serve it with custard, cream or ice cream! If you have any left over, it's great eaten cold the next day, just cover and keep it in the fridge.

1. Preheat the oven to 200°C/180°C fan.

2. In a small bowl, mix together the caster sugar and half the cinnamon.

3. Unroll the pastry on to a baking tray lined with baking paper. Score a 2cm border around the edges of the pastry with a knife, making sure you don't cut all the way through it. Prick inside the border all over with a fork.

4. Brush all over with the beaten egg, then scatter over half the cinnamon sugar.

5. Bake for about 20 minutes until golden and crispy.

6. Meanwhile, melt the butter in a large non-stick frying pan over a medium heat.

7. Add the apples, sultanas, lemon zest and juice, muscovado sugar and remaining cinnamon to the pan. Stir and cook for 15–20 minutes until the apples are nice and tender and most of the liquid has evaporated.

8. When the pastry is cooked, use the back of a spoon to press down inside the border to make space for the apple filling.

9. Pour the hot apple filling on to the pastry inside the border, sprinkle over the pecans and the remaining cinnamon sugar, then cut into slices and serve with custard, cream or ice cream.

Summer Strawberry & Raspberry Crumble

Serves 6–8 / 40 minutes

300g strawberries
300g raspberries
100g light muscovado or
    caster sugar
100g ground almonds
175g plain flour
75g cold butter, diced
100g flaked almonds

Clotted cream, to serve

This crumble is a perfect summer dessert. The recipe comes from one of my best mates and is something we always have round his house after dinner. I love the sweet, cakey layer the ground almonds give between the fruit and crumble. Serve it warm with a good dollop of clotted cream. Bliss!

1. Preheat the oven to 200°C/180°C fan.

2. Remove the stalks from the strawberries and cut any larger ones in half. Put the strawberries and raspberries into an ovenproof dish. Scatter over 1 tbsp of the sugar, then scatter over the ground almonds.

3. Put the flour and butter into a mixing bowl. Use your fingertips to rub the butter into the flour until it resembles breadcrumbs, then stir in the remaining sugar and flaked almonds.

4. Scatter the mixture evenly over the fruit.

5. Bake for 30–35 minutes until lightly golden.

6. Serve with clotted cream.

Pictured on p. 190–1

White Chocolate, Cranberry & Pistachio Biscotti

Makes 24 / 1 hour

175g plain flour, plus extra
  for dusting
150g caster sugar
1 tsp baking powder
75g pistachios, chopped
75g white chocolate chips
75g dried cranberries
2 eggs, lightly beaten
Pinch of salt

One of the best dunkers around! Biscotti means twice baked, making this Italian sweet treat nice and crispy. You can play around with the flavours here using different chocolate and nuts. If you pop them in a fancy box or bag, they make a lovely gift at Christmas. Keep them sealed in biscuit tin and they will last a good week!

1. Preheat the oven to 200°C/180°C fan.

2. Line 2 baking trays with baking paper.

3. Sift the flour into a mixing bowl, stir in the sugar and baking powder, then stir in the nuts, chocolate chips and cranberries.

4. Add the eggs a little at a time, mixing with your hand until the mixture comes together to form a dough. The dough should not be sticky; you may not need all of the egg. Add a little flour if it becomes too sticky.

5. Divide the dough into 2 balls, then roll each one into a 20cm sausage on a lightly floured work surface.

6. Place each dough sausage on a prepared baking tray and bake for 20 minutes.

7. Remove from the oven and leave to cool for 10 minutes.

8. Reduce the oven temperature to 160°C/140°C fan.

9. Use a bread knife to gently cut the dough sausages into 1cm slices.

10. Place the slices back on to the trays, cut-side down. Bake for 15 minutes until crisp. Leave to cool on the tray or a wire rack before serving.

Pictured on p. 194–5

Rhubarb Eton Mess

Makes 4 / 30–35 minutes

6 sticks of rhubarb, cut into
  2cm pieces
1 large orange
2 tbsp honey, plus extra
  to serve
300ml double cream
1 tbsp caster sugar
1 tbsp vanilla bean paste
  or extract
4 shop-bought meringue nests

I remember eating sticks of rhubarb dipped in sugar with my dad when I was a kid. I love the stuff. In 2021, I was lucky enough to visit a farmer that produces rhubarb in the Wye Valley. He gave me a load to take home and said his favourite way to cook it was with some orange and it really works. Since then, it's become a staple combo in my Eton mess, and if you've never tried rhubarb before, then this is a delicious place to start.

1. Put the rhubarb into a small saucepan with the juice of the orange and the honey. Cook over a medium heat for 5–10 minutes until the rhubarb has softened and you are left with a syrupy sauce. Taste and if it's too sour, then add more honey to sweeten. Leave to cool for 15 minutes.

2. Using the fine side of a grater or zester, remove the orange zest into a large mixing bowl, then add the cream, sugar and vanilla.

3. Use a hand whisk or electric whisk to beat the cream until it is thick and just holds its shape.

4. When the rhubarb is cool, crumble 3 of the meringues into the cream, add half the rhubarb and gently fold together with a large spoon.

5. Divide the mixture into 4 serving bowls or glasses. Crumble over the remaining meringue, top with the remaining rhubarb and drizzle with honey.

Simple Chocolate Fondants

Makes 4 / 20–25 minutes

175g unsalted butter, diced
2 tbsp cocoa powder
125g 70% dark chocolate,
  chopped
100g caster sugar
1 tsp vanilla extract
2 eggs, plus 2 egg yolks
50g plain flour

Cream or vanilla ice cream,
  to serve

Pure gooey, chocolatey indulgence. This is a show-stopping pud that's a real treat to order out but is easy to make at home too. These fondants can also be served as molten chocolate pots – just leave them in the ramekins and dive in with your spoon.

1. Preheat the oven to 200°C/180°C fan.

2. Use 50g of the butter to grease the inside of 4 small ramekins. Add some cocoa to each ramekin. Tip the ramekin around so the inside is evenly coated in cocoa, then tap out any excess.

3. Put the chocolate and remaining butter into a small pan over a low heat and stir for a couple of minutes until melted. Turn off the heat and set aside.

4. Add the sugar, vanilla, eggs and egg yolks to a mixing bowl. Whisk for 2 minutes until light and pale. Add the flour and stir with a spoon until combined.

5. Pour the melted chocolate and butter mixture into the egg mix. Stir until you have a smooth, even-coloured batter.

6. Divide the batter into the ramekins, leaving 1cm at the top as they will rise slightly during cooking.

7. Bake for about 10 minutes until the tops begin to form a crust.

8. Remove from the oven and leave to cool for 1–2 minutes.

9. To turn them out, hold a hot ramekin with a tea towel or oven glove. Put the serving plate on top, then flip it over and gently remove the ramekin. Repeat with the remaining ramekins.

10. Serve with a drizzle of cream or drop a scoop of ice cream on top.

Chocolate & Raspberry Brownie

Serves 12 / 1 hour 15 minutes

5 tbsp raspberry jam
250g butter
100g cocoa powder
300g caster sugar
3 eggs, beaten with 1 tbsp
  vanilla bean paste
75g plain flour
Pinch of salt
100g raspberries

This might just be the best brownie around. With this recipe, you get that lovely crispy top with a fudgy middle and the slight sharpness of the raspberries works a treat with the rich, gooey chocolate. Cut it up to serve as a teatime treat, or for a fuss-free dinner party pud, slice it into wedges and serve with a dollop of crème fraîche, a few raspberries and a little sprig of mint. Keep wrapped and it will last for up to 5 days.

1. Preheat the oven to 200°C/180°C fan.

2. Grease and line a 24cm cake tin with greaseproof paper.

3. Put the jam and butter into a large saucepan over a medium heat and stir until melted. Remove from the heat.

4. Sift in the cocoa, then add the sugar, stirring with a wooden spoon until well combined.

5. Slowly pour in the eggs and vanilla, stirring as you go until you have a smooth mixture.

6. Sift in the flour and salt. Mix gently until combined into a smooth mixture. Stir in the raspberries.

7. Pour into the cake tin and bake for 20 minutes, then reduce the oven temperature to 180°C/160°C fan and bake for a further 30–40 minutes or until a skewer inserted into the centre comes out clean.

8. Place the tin on a wire rack and leave to cool completely before removing from the tin and serving as you wish.

Ultimate Chocolate Chip Cookies

Makes 10–12 / **25 minutes, *plus 30 minutes chilling***

100g unsalted butter
150g caster sugar
75g light muscovado sugar
1 egg
2 tsp vanilla extract
175g plain flour
Pinch of salt
100g 70% dark chocolate,
  broken into small chunks

For me, the perfect cookie has to have a crisp, crunchy edge with a soft, chewy, melting chocolate middle and that is what we have right here. The smell you get when they are baking is insane, but don't be tempted to pull them out of the oven before they're done! Luckily, you won't have to wait long as these are best served slightly warm. They will keep for a few days too, and you don't need a fancy mixer to make them either!

1. Preheat the oven to 200°C/180°C fan.

2. Line 2 baking trays with baking paper.

3. Melt the butter in a saucepan or in a heatproof bowl in the microwave.

4. Put both sugars into a mixing bowl, pour in the melted butter and beat with a wooden spoon for 5–8 minutes until lighter in colour with a slightly fluffy texture.

5. Add the egg and vanilla and mix until combined.

6. Add the flour and salt and mix until a dough just forms, then stir in the chocolate. Transfer to the fridge to chill for 30 minutes.

7. Divide the dough into 10–12 balls, depending on how big you want your cookies, and place them on the prepared baking trays, leaving a few inches of space between each one as they will spread during cooking.

8. Press each ball down with your fingers to flatten slightly.

9. Bake for 10–11 minutes until slightly golden – they will still be soft when they come out of the oven.

10. Leave to cool on the trays for 20 minutes before serving.

Index

Note: page numbers in *italics* refer to illustrations.